Electric Guitar
HANDBOOK

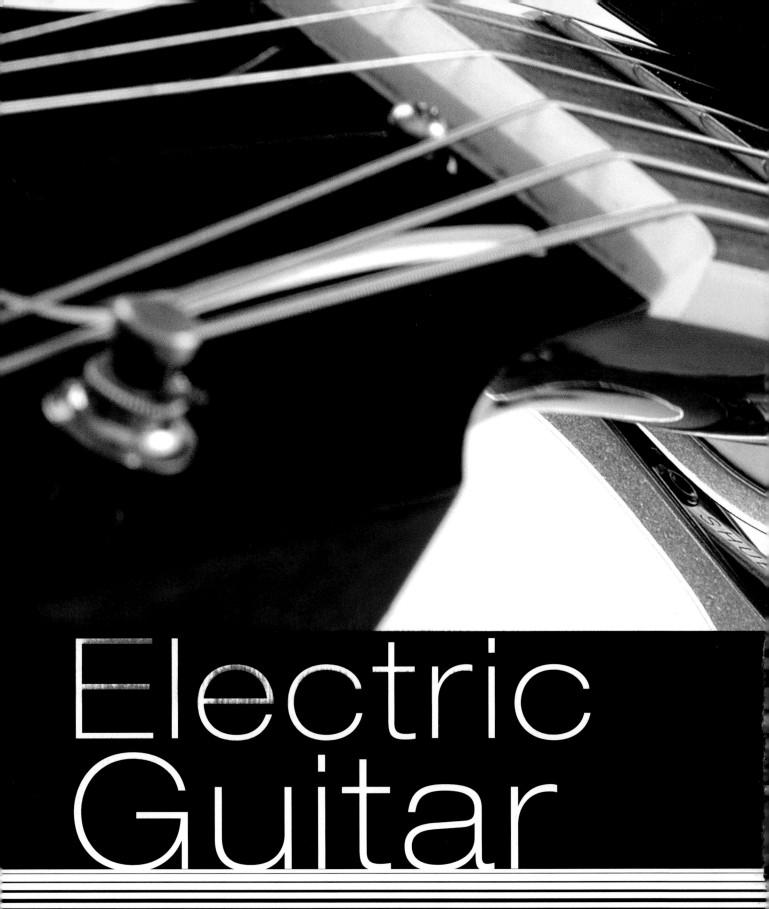

Electric
Guitar
HANDBOOK

ALAN RATCLIFFE

First published in 2005 by New Holland (Publishers) Ltd
London • Cape Town • Sydney • Auckland
www.newhollandpublishers.com

Garfield House	80 McKenzie St	14 Aquatic Drive	218 Lake Rd
86 Edgware Rd	Cape Town	Frenchs Forest NSW	Northcote
London W2 2EA	8001	2086	Auckland
United Kingdom	South Africa	Australia	New Zealand

PUBLISHER & EDITOR Mariëlle Renssen
PUBLISHING MANAGERS Claudia Dos Santos & Simon Pooley
COMMISSIONING EDITOR Alfred LeMaitre
DESIGNER Geraldine Cupido
ILLUSTRATIONS James Berrangé
PICTURE RESEARCHER Karla Kik
PRODUCTION Myrna Collins
PROOFREADER Elizabeth Wilson
CONSULTANT Mark A Greenwood

ISBN 1 84537 042 2 (hardback)
ISBN 1 84537 043 0 (paperback)

Reproduction by Resolution Colour (Pty) Ltd, Cape Town
Printed in Malaysia by Times Offset (M) Sdn. Bhd.

1 3 5 7 9 10 8 6 4 2

Contents

CHAPTER 1

The Electric GUITAR

The Rickenbacker 'Frying Pan' electric Hawaiian guitar was the first true electric guitar.

EVOLUTION OF THE ELECTRIC GUITAR

As early as 1925 American George Beauchamp, one of the founders of the National String Instrument Company, experimented with electromagnetic pick-ups to capture the sound of the strings and convert it to an electric signal, which could be amplified with the aid of the radio and hi-fi amplifiers of the day. After designing and making a working pick-up, Beauchamp fixed it in 1931 to a Hawaiian guitar body and took the prototype — nicknamed the 'Frying Pan' — to Adolph Rickenbacker, who was manufacturing metal bodies for National. Together they formed the Rickenbacker Company and started manufacturing the electric Hawaiian guitars in 1932.

Lloyd Loar was an acoustical engineer for Gibson Mandolin-Guitar Manufacturing Co. Ltd., established by New York-born mandolin and guitar player, Orville Gibson. Loar was known for his contributions to the design of the mandolin, and had been experimenting with electrical amplification of the guitar since the early 1920s.

In 1933 he created a new company, Vivi-Tone (a division of Gibson), exclusively producing Spanish-style electric guitars. Due to the poor design of the instrument and, at the time,

The driving force behind the early development of the electric guitar can be summed up in one word: volume. In the 1920s, guitarists playing with Big Band and Swing orchestras were being drowned out by other instruments, and needed louder guitars to help make themselves heard.

The basic difference between acoustic and electric guitars is the way the sound is amplified. An acoustic guitar uses a mechanical device, the soundbox, while the electric guitar uses an electromagnetic pick-up and an electronic amplifier. Generally, the differences between the two guitars are not as great as the contrasts in tone and design would lead you to believe. Both instruments are played by striking the strings with the right hand while choosing the notes to be sounded with the left. The tuning and the position of the notes are identical on both instruments, and any piece of music which can be played on one can also be played on the other.

In terms of the body shape, the acoustic guitar, whether in its steel- or nylon-string version, is dictated by the soundbox, where a small variation in shape or size can radically affect the tone or volume of the instrument. Electric guitars do not suffer such constraints, and their designers have much more freedom in deciding the size and shape of the body.

right *First made in 1936, the Gibson ES-150 was the first commercially successful Spanish-style electric guitar.*

Charlie Christian, an inventive jazz soloist with the Benny Goodman Sextet, here with his Gibson ES-150. Its success as the first modern electric guitar was largely due to Christian.

too small a market to sustain a company with only one product, Vivi-Tone failed within a year.

In 1935 Gibson commissioned a well-known slide guitarist, Alvino Rey, to help develop a new guitar pick-up which was first used on a lap steel guitar in 1935. By 1936 this pick-up was introduced on a standard 'f-hole' arch-top guitar — designated the Gibson ES-150 — which we now recognize as being the first modern electric guitar. Guitarists adopted the instrument wholeheartedly, making it an instant success. A new style of guitar playing developed, spearheaded by Charlie Christian, the guitarist with the Benny Goodman Sextet. This style used the extra volume of the electric guitar to good effect, allowing him to solo in a way that previously only horn players had been able to do. The Gibson ES-150 is still known as the 'Charlie Christian' model, while the pick-up is referred to as 'the Christian' in his honour.

left *The original Fender Telecaster, designed by Leo Fender, was the first production solid-body electric guitar.*

SOLID BODY GUITARS

Even though the ES-150 was a commercial success, it still had some problems. Due to the hollow body and microphonic pick-ups, it was prone to feedback and undesirable overtones as it picked up as much of the body sound as that produced by the strings. The well-known American jazz guitarist Les Paul, reasoning that a solid body was the solution to these problems, made his own simple pick-ups, and designed and built a prototype from a 10x10cm (4x4in) plank of pine and a Gibson neck. He affectionately called this prototype 'the Log'. To make the Log look more like a guitar, Paul glued two sides sawn from a hollow-body guitar to it. In 1946, happy with the reduced feedback and overtones of his prototype, Paul took the Log to the Gibson company, which was unconvinced that it would sell and declined to manufacture his solid-body electric guitar.

However, Leo Fender, a radio repairman, believed in the future of the solid-body electric guitar. In 1943 he built a prototype from oak, which he rented out to musicians. The feedback he got from them he used to improve his designs, and in 1948 he released his Broadcaster guitar. The Fender Broadcaster was soon renamed 'the Telecaster', since the musical instrument company Gretsch had a drum kit called Broadcaster. Aside from the long sustain, resistance to feedback and lack of unwanted overtones exhibited by Les Paul's Log, Leo Fender's instrument had a number of

unique features and innovations that made it special. The neck and fingerboard were one piece of maple, which was detachable to make servicing or replacement easier, in addition to being simpler and cheaper to manufacture; an asymmetric headstock with all the machine heads on one side made tuning easier and let the strings run through the nut in a relatively straight line; and adjustable bridge saddles allowed for the intonation, action and bridge radius to be adjusted.

Partly as a result of the success of Fender's Telecaster, Gibson finally designed and built a high-quality solid-body electric guitar in 1952. While the finished product was called the Les Paul, the design came from

The original Gibson Les Paul was designed by Gibson's Ted McCarty – but inspired by Les Paul.

Gibson's president, Ted McCarty, and was based more on older Gibson guitars than on the ES-150 or the Log. The body was mahogany with a carved maple top finished in gold, the mahogany neck with its ebony fingerboard was glued in, and the pick-ups were P-90 — or 'soapbar' — pick-ups, which were highly versatile and warm sounding. To increase the sustain, the Les Paul was a very heavy guitar. The Les Paul was very successful from 1952 to 1961, when lagging sales prompted new innovations.

BB King with the semihollow-body Gibson ES-335, which produced a combination of warm tones and good sound quality.

Introducing innovations

In 1954 Fender introduced the Stratocaster, which was to become the most popular (and most copied) electric guitar in history. Once again utilizing feedback from leading musicians of the time, the Fender Stratocaster was designed with a number of new features that made it futuristic for its time. The body was an offset double-cutaway with 'custom contour' — the cutaways and bevelled edges made the guitar very comfortable to hold and play. Three pick-ups and a unique set of electronics gave the guitar a wide range of tones.

The Stratocaster also featured a vibrato bridge, designed to 'bend' notes (change the pitch of a note) or apply vibrato with the right hand. The vibrato bridge, called a 'tremolo' by Fender, allowed for individual height and

left *The Fender Stratocaster, the symbol of rock'n'roll, spawned a legion of imitations.*

intonation adjustment for each string, enabling action, intonation and even radius to be set. The period 1958 to 1961 was an exciting time for guitar making. The Les Paul was outfitted with 'humbucking' pick-ups — more powerful pick-ups which effectively cancelled any hum (hence 'humbucker') by using two coils. This instrument had four different models: the Les Paul Junior, Special, Standard and Custom.

During this time, Gibson also released the ES-335, which was the first semihollow-body guitar. With hollow sides and a solid centre block where the pick-ups and neck were mounted, the ES-335 combined the warm tones of a traditional hollow guitar with the better sound quality of a solid guitar.

In 1958 and 1959, Gibson also introduced a series of futuristic guitars such as the Flying V and the Explorer. Unfortunately these were not very successful until heavy metal music made them popular in the 1970s and 1980s. In 1961, the SG (Solid Guitar) series was introduced to take over from the then discontinued Les Paul guitars.

Frank Zappa playing his Gibson SG – the successor to the Les Paul with a thin body and a double cutaway.

and a Floyd Rose tremolo bridge. The next true guitar innovator was the engineer Ned Steinberger, who in 1982 produced a guitar with a very small graphite fibre-resin body and no headstock. Tuning was carried out by tuning machines on the bridge of the guitar. Also making their debut on the Steinberger guitars were EMG active pick-ups. These guitars had a very even tonal response due to the synthetic materials used. Unfortunately, once the novelty wore off, most guitarists decided they preferred the idiosyncrasies and tonal characteristics of wood.

Another radical design was the Parker Fly. Designed by Ken Parker with the piezo pick-up system (see pp18–19) by Larry Fishman (of Fishman Transducers), this guitar was introduced in 1993. It features a very thin, contoured wooden body for tone and a synthetic exoskeleton for strength and stability. The 24-fret neck has a synthetic fingerboard and stainless steel frets, both of which are extremely durable. The bridge saddles each contain a piezo element that picks up a very 'acoustic' type of sound directly from the strings, then onboard electronics enable this to be blended with the electromagnetic pick-up sound.

The majority of innovations for the next few decades were the result of specialized companies catering for musicians who wanted to modify or improve their factory standard instruments. Pick-up companies such as DiMarzio and Seymour Duncan started making replacement pick-ups that were more powerful or offered a different tone to the standard production models. Musician-inventor Floyd Rose and the Kahler company both designed tremolos that could be used for radical bending and yet would remain completely in tune. Some newer Japanese companies such as Ibanez, Yamaha and Aria started introducing these retrofit features on production models which, coupled with lower prices, gave these manufacturers a foothold in the industry.

In 1982 the American company Charvel Jackson introduced the Soloist, which was the first 'Superstrat' guitar. The Soloist shape was similar to a Stratocaster, but with extended cutaways which allowed easy access to the highest notes on the 24-fret through-neck. Also standard features were a humbucker at the bridge position

right *The Parker Fly utilizes a combination of traditional wood and modern synthetic materials.*

Anatomy of the electric guitar

1. Tuning machines
Also called tuners or machine heads; these change the tension, thus tuning, of strings.

2. Headstock
Holds the tuning machines. Most often arranged on the headstock in a three-a-side (3+3) configuration or with all six on one side (6+0).

3. Nut
Establishes both spacing and height of strings above the frets. Can be considered the 'zero' fret as it is where strings' 'speaking length' starts.

4. Neck
Made from harder woods for stability and to resist warping, and shaped to be comfortable for the fretting hand.

5. Fingerboard
Sometimes called the fretboard, it is the playing surface of the neck where frets are placed. Two important factors are radius and type of wood.

6. Frets
Strips of metal that run across the neck. They divide the strings into shorter lengths to determine specific notes when the string is held down (fretted).

7. Truss rod
Adjustable steel rod set into neck below fingerboard to help counter tension of steel strings.

8. Neck joint
Method used to join the guitar neck to the body.

9. Scale length
Length of string from where it leaves nut to point it makes contact with saddle (bridge), i.e. the whole 'speaking length' of the string.

10. Pick-ups
These sense mechanical vibration of the strings, and convert it into electrical energy which can then be changed by means of effects and amplified.

11. Body shape
Not simply cosmetic; some elements of the shape will affect playability or comfort.

12. Cutaways
If body is cut away where it joins neck, it makes access to the upper frets of the neck easier.

13. Body contour
Guitar body is sculpted to make it fit more comfortably with the human body.

14. Scratchplate (pick guard)
(Not illustrated.) Protects guitar body from scratching by fingers and plectra. Found on many instruments such as the Fender Stratocaster; this is also used to attach pick-ups, and volume and tone controls to the guitar.

15. Bridge
Holds ends of the strings in place. Tremolo bridges can also add vibrato.

16. Pick-up selector switch

Switches between pick-ups and combinations of
pick-ups to create a variety of sounds.

17. Volume controls

Used to vary output level of a pick-up or even of
the whole guitar.

18. Tone controls

Cut (reduce) treble frequencies in the signal as
the control is turned down.

19. Output socket

Jack plug socket where signal leaves the guitar.

20. Strap buttons

Used to attach a strap to
the guitar.

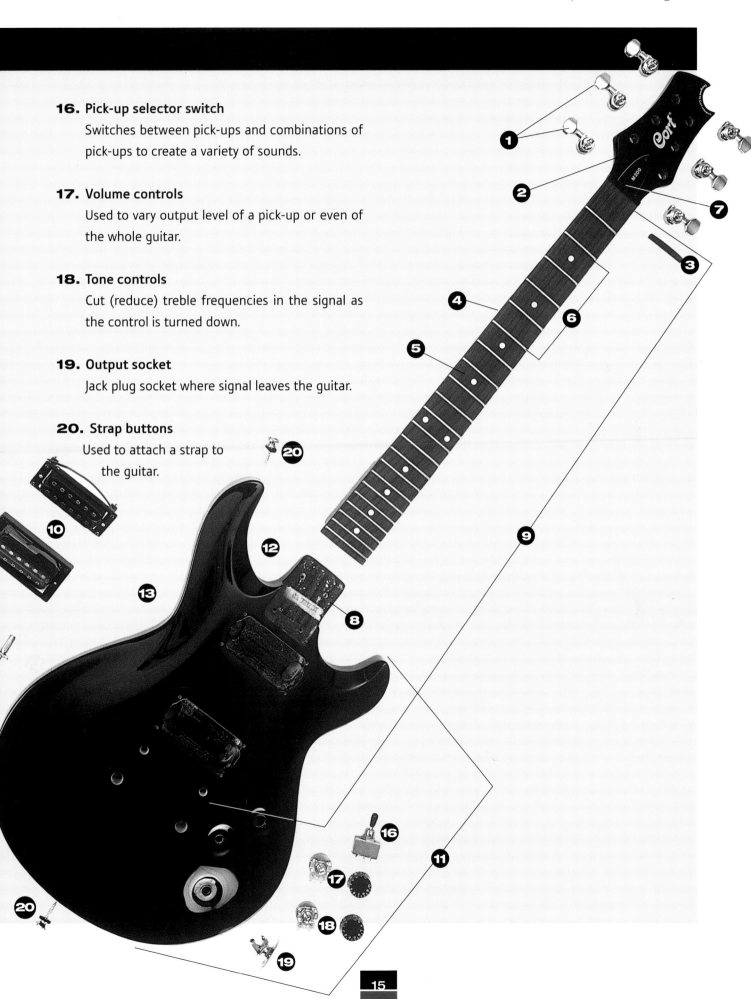

NEW TECHNOLOGY

Early guitar designs such as the Fender Telecaster and Stratocaster as well as the Gibson Les Paul and ES-335 have been amazingly durable, with few changes since their creation. This is testament to the thoroughness and foresight of the pioneers who designed them. However, advances in manufacturing techniques and electronics as well as the advent of space-age materials have enabled a new breed of innovators to introduce refinements to the basic designs, materials and manufacturing of electric guitars, as well as create some stunningly innovative instruments.

A set of EMG SA single-coil active pick-ups, which are low-impedance designs with preamplifiers built in.

ACTIVE PICK-UPS

These use very low-impedance coils made with very few turns of wire; this makes them low-powered but hum-resistant. They also usually have low-power magnets to avoid 'string pull'. While either of these factors would usually make for an unusably quiet pick-up, the active pick-up has a preamplifier built into it that boosts it to the same, or even higher, levels than a passive (conventional) pick-up. As a result of the low impedance, a guitar with active pick-ups is not prone to as much hum or other noise (even the single-coil models) as conventional designs. The wiring and even the cable used is also less prone to interference and noise.

Many guitarists like the brighter, clearer sound of active pick-ups and feel that they work best for applications where a lot of effects are used. Others feel that they have a slightly compressed sound with less dynamic range than pas-

sive pick-ups. The disadvantage of active pick-ups is that they require power to run the preamplifiers and can't be used without batteries or other power sources.

MIDI GUITAR & GUITAR SYNTHESIZERS

MIDI (Musical Instrument Digital Interface) is the standardized language which allows any digital musical device to talk to another. Originally developed to allow different keyboard synthesizers to play each other's sounds, it has grown to the point where virtually every hi-tech musical device has some sort of MIDI control.

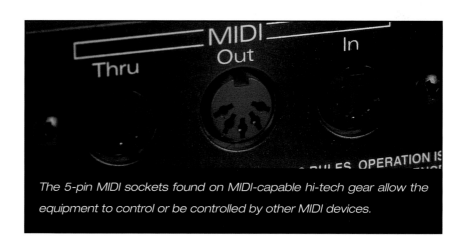

The 5-pin MIDI sockets found on MIDI-capable hi-tech gear allow the equipment to control or be controlled by other MIDI devices.

MIDI guitar systems

This system translates the note information from a guitar into MIDI, allowing you to control MIDI devices such as synthesizers. In its most basic form it consists of a guitar, a hexaphonic (hex) pick-up (see right) and a guitar-to-MIDI converter. Of course, you still need a MIDI device such as a keyboard synthesizer or a sound module to turn the MIDI data into sounds.

While early systems forced the player to use a special guitar, modern systems allow you to use virtually any guitar. Some major companies such as Fender and Brian Moore are now manufacturing guitars with hex pick-up systems built in. These are often called Roland Ready (RR), as Roland are the most popular manufacturer of MIDI guitar systems. It is worth noting that the Roland VG guitar modelling systems, which also use hex pick-ups, are not MIDI guitar systems.

HEXAPHONIC PICK-UPS

These feature six pick-ups in one package (one pick-up for each string). Most also have some controls to govern parameters such as program changes and synthesizer volume. There are three common types of hex pick-up you are likely to encounter.

External electromagnetic These are the most common type and attach externally to the guitar. The pick-ups are electromagnetic and there is usually a separate box with controls and a 13-pin output socket. They require no permanent modification of the guitar, and as such are good for the player just getting into the MIDI guitar world. However, they do not work quite as well as the piezo hex pick-ups, need to be well positioned and are relatively unattractive due to the box with the controls on.

The Fender RR Stratocaster has a built-in hex pick-up system for driving guitar synthesizers.

The Roland GK-2A hexaphonic pick-up can be added to almost any electric guitar.

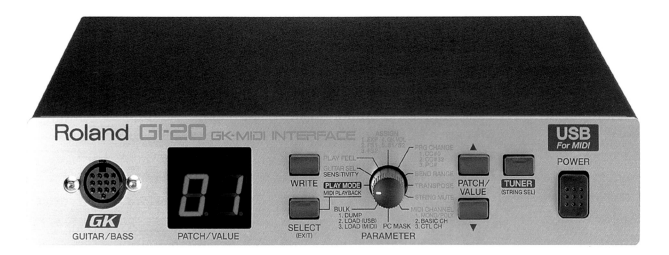

Internal electromagnetic The same as the external, but made to fit most of the electronics inside the guitar. They are less obtrusive than external versions, but the guitar does require modifying for them to fit.

Internal piezo Piezo pick-ups are built into the bridge saddles of the guitar, and the electronics are internal. They work very well and also give a usable piezo output (sounds very similar to an acoustic guitar). They are unobtrusive, but still require guitar modification.

Guitar-to-MIDI converters

This is the main component of a MIDI guitar system. It takes the signal from the hex pick-up and outputs

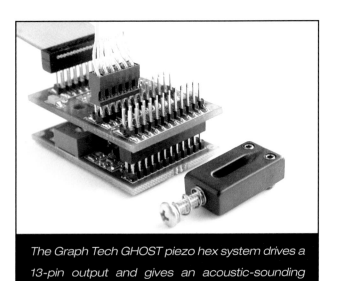

The Graph Tech GHOST piezo hex system drives a 13-pin output and gives an acoustic-sounding piezo output.

above *The Roland GI-20 guitar-to-MIDI converter converts the output from a 13-pin hex pick-up into MIDI.*

conventional MIDI data playable by any MIDI-capable synthesizer. It does this by identifying the notes played and generating MIDI note information with the same values. It is done independently for each string to minimize errors — which is why a hex pick-up is used. Since the guitar note must sound before it can be recognized and converted, there is always a short delay, especially noticeable on the lower notes.

Guitar synthesizers

These combine the guitar-to-MIDI converter and a synthesizer in one package. Guitar synthesizers are convenient for gigging but limited soundwise.

Any upgrade means changing everything except the hex pick-up.

MODELLING GUITARS

These also use a hexaphonic pick-up and controls, similar to MIDI guitar applications. The idea with guitar modelling is to get a simple signal from each string, which can then be modified by electronics to 'model' a particular guitar sound.

The sound modelled can be that of any type of guitar, played through any combination of amplifier and speakers. The sound can also include finer details such

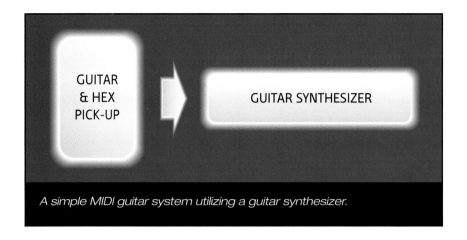

A simple MIDI guitar system utilizing a guitar synthesizer.

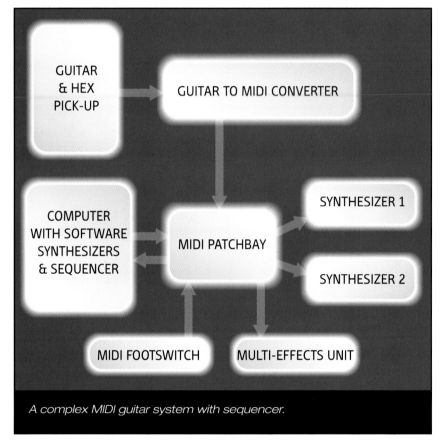

A complex MIDI guitar system with sequencer.

PIEZO SADDLES

This is a spin-off of the acoustic guitar pick-up industry, where a strip containing small piezoelectric crystals (which, when stressed, produce electricity) is fitted under the saddle. These pick-ups are highly feedback-resistant as they pick up most of their sound directly from the strings, and have a very good high-frequency response which ensures that they still sound very acoustic.

It later became evident that piezo crystals embedded in the saddle of an electric guitar would also give a fairly good acoustic sound. This led to piezo saddles being used in hex pick-up systems for MIDI guitar and for modelling systems. Manufacturers are now producing a variety of replacement piezo saddles and bridges specifically for electric guitars.

SYNTHETIC MATERIALS

The best known example of modern synthetic materials used is the carbon fibre body and neck of Steinberger guitars and basses. There are many other areas, however, where they've been used too.

as the type of pick-ups used, as well as type and positioning of microphones. As a result of the separate string processing, alternate tunings and even emulation of instruments such as 12-string acoustic guitars can be programmed.

This gives the player the ability to change instantly from a nylon-string acoustic-guitar sound to a Fender Stratocaster played through a Fender Twin Reverb amplifier at the touch of a switch!

Carbon fibre is often used for the support rods in bass guitar necks, allowing maximum stiffness without adding weight. Graph Tech have produced synthetic nuts and saddles that sound similar to vintage ivory, and others that are self-lubricating with many times less friction than graphite.

Parker uses a synthetic exoskeleton for its guitars, making them strong but at the same time leaving them very light and resonant.

THE GREAT GUITARS
FENDER TELECASTER

The Telecaster has the distinction of being the first mass-produced solid-body electric guitar, and was quite a revolutionary instrument for its time. Introduced in 1948 by Fender as the Broadcaster, the name was soon changed to the Telecaster as Gretsch had a drum kit called the Broadcaster.

The bolt-on neck was fixed to the body by means of four screws; it could be replaced quickly or removed for repairs. It had a 65cm (25½in) scale length and 21 frets, joining the body at the 17th fret. Both the neck and fingerboard were originally made from one piece of maple, with the truss rod (introduced in 1949) installed from the rear and covered with a dark strip of Hawaiian koa (sometimes called the 'skunk stripe'). Later Telecasters were made with a rosewood fingerboard and the truss rod was installed under the fingerboard. Today both types of fingerboard are available. The machine heads are all on one side of the asymmetric headstock, which enables the strings to run through the nut in a relatively straight line.

The flat, solid body is made either of ash or alder and has a single cutaway. The strings are mounted from the rear of the guitar, running first through the body and bridge, then over the saddle and up the neck. The bridge originally had a cover, which most players removed as they found it got in the way. It also featured three adjustable saddles, each serving two strings, which could be moved up or down for action adjustments as well as toward or away from the neck for setting the intonation. On newer Telecasters the three saddles have been replaced with six to allow for

The Fender Telecaster, introduced in 1948 as the Broadcaster, featured a bolt-on neck and a single cutaway.

individual intonation-setting, as with the Stratocaster. The Telecaster has two single-coil pick-ups. The neck pick-up has a metal cover and base plate to reduce electrical interference and is screwed directly into the wood of the body; the bridge pick-up also has a metal base plate but is suspended from the metal bridge. The controls consist of a volume and a tone control, with pick-up selection being handled by a three-way switch. They are mounted on a metal plate which screws onto the body.

The Telecaster is still a very popular instrument, especially among country and pop players, and valued for its clear, trebly tone and well-defined articulation.

FENDER STRATOCASTER

The Stratocaster is arguably the most influential instrument of all time. It is the most copied electric guitar and is still one of the most sought-after. Introduced by Fender in 1954, the Stratocaster shared

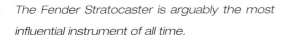

some features with the Telecaster: a similar asymmetric headstock, the 65cm (25½in) scale length bolt-on maple neck and single-coil pick-ups. However, as with the Telecaster, there was much that was new and revolutionary: the body, while still being made from ash or alder, sported two cutaways and was contoured at the back and under the armrest to fit the player's body. The scratch-plate was larger and supported the controls and pick-ups. There were three single-coil pick-ups selected by a three-way switch (one pick-up at a time). The three-way was later changed to a five-way switch, adding the options of bridge and middle pick-up together, or middle and neck pick-ups together. A master volume control and two tone controls (one each for the neck and middle pick-ups) were positioned near the player's right hand. The output jack plug socket was recessed and mounted on the front face of the guitar.

The bridge now had six individually adjustable saddles and featured a radically new design for a vibrato (called 'tremolo' by Fender), where the whole bridge itself pivoted instead of having the more usual separate bridge and tremolo unit.

The neck was from one piece of maple, with a maple fingerboard; the headstock was reshaped to make it more attractive than the Telecaster; and the fingerboard had 22 frets, with the neck joining the body at the 16th fret.

Although the Stratocaster has stayed basically the same instrument from 1954 until now, Fender does

offer variations with a variety of features that differ from the standard models. It is still popular with players of all styles and ages.

GIBSON LES PAUL STANDARD

In 1952, in response to the success of the Fender Broadcaster/Telecaster, Gibson took Les Paul's advice and designed a high-quality, solid-body electric guitar. With a contoured carved top, 'trapeze' tailpiece, glue-in neck, traditional single-cutaway shape, and bound neck and body, the design was based more on classic Gibson guitars than on the company's newer, hollow-bodied electric models.

The top was maple, finished with gold, while the body and 62cm (24½in) scale length neck were mahogany. The pick-ups were P-90 (also called 'soap bar') single-coil models controlled by a three-way selector switch and with a volume and tone control for each pick-up. The control cavity was rear-routed and had a plastic cover.

In 1954 the new Tune-O-Matic bridge, which had individual intonation adjustment and a separate tailpiece, replaced the original trapeze tailpiece.

Then, in 1957, the pick-ups were changed to humbuckers and in 1958 the finish was changed to a classic sunburst — the modern Gibson Les Paul Standard was born.

One other variant of the Les Paul well worth noting is the Les Paul Custom. While basically the same instrument as the Standard, the hardware is all

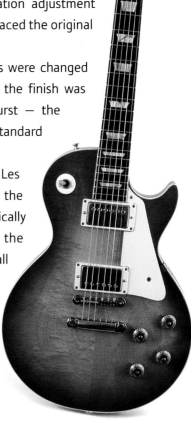

gold and the finish either solid black or solid white, resulting in a very classy-looking instrument.

Because of flagging sales, the Les Paul was discontinued in 1960, but was reintroduced in 1968 as interest again blossomed. Thanks to the thick mahogany body, glued-in neck and humbucking pick-ups, the Gibson Les Paul has a long sustain and a darker tone than the Fender guitars. The shorter scale length produces a softer action when set up correctly. It is still popular in rock, hard rock and metal circles — and its darker tone makes it popular among jazz players, too.

Gibson SG

The Gibson SG (Solid Guitar) was the replacement for the Les Paul, introduced the same year (1960) the Les Paul was discontinued. While keeping the same pick-up, bridge and controls, the mahogany body is much thinner and lighter, with a double cutaway, and does not have the carved maple top.

The 22-fret neck is mahogany, and the fretboard is rosewood, joining the body at the 21st fret and making upper fret access effortless.

The Gibson SG is popular among rock and blues-rock musicians — and for those who want a lighter, more playable guitar with the Gibson sound.

Gibson ES-335

First made by Gibson in 1958, the ES-335 is something of a hybrid. While the hollow body is similar to those preceding it, there is a solid block of wood running down the centre of the guitar on which the neck, bridge and pick-ups are mounted. This centre block

The Gibson SG, originally introduced to replace the Les Paul, is a very thin guitar and has quite an aggressive tone.

The semi-hollow Gibson ES-355 has a solid centre block which makes it more resistant to feedback than hollow-bodied instruments.

helps to stabilize the guitar, reducing feedback and improving sustain. The hollow body adds some of the resonance and character which solid-body guitars lack. Made from laminated maple, a slender body features a double cutaway and two ornamental f-holes. The 62cm (24½in) scale length mahogany neck has a 22-fret rosewood fingerboard which joins the body at the 20th fret. The familiar Tune-O-Matic bridge, two humbuckers, three-way switch and four pot (potentiometer) controls are also featured.

The ES-335 has for many years been a favourite of blues, rock, rock'n'roll and jazz players, particularly where volume levels are relatively high but more resonance is desired.

Rickenbacker 360-12

Rickenbacker electric guitars are known for their unique sound — a glassy 'jangle' that's distinctly different from the tone of either Fender or Gibson guitars. The 360-12 is the 12-string version of the semihollow, electric Rickenbacker model 360.

The 360-12 was made famous by George Harrison of The Beatles, Roger McGuinn of The Byrds and Tom Petty of Tom Petty and the Heartbreakers.

Paul Reed Smith guitars are modern classics which are built to very high standards, using exceptional quality woods.

PAUL REED SMITH (PRS)

PRS is a manufacturer of high-quality electric guitars based loosely on the Gibson Les Paul with their mahogany bodies and necks, and carved maple tops. However, most PRS guitars have double cutaways and rotary pick-up selector switches.

The scale length of PRS guitars falls between that of Fender and Gibson at 64cm (25in). This makes the action softer than the Fender guitars; also, PRS guitars have slightly stiffer string tension and better articulation than Gibson instruments. Most models feature high-quality figured woods and inlay work. A PRS signature is the natural wood binding, where the edges of the maple cap are natural unstained wood in contrast with the darker mahogany backs and stained-top finishes.

The Rickenbacker 360-12 is the most sought-after electric 12-string guitar and has a distinctive jangling tone.

The Ibanez Universe, developed with guitarist Steve Vai, has a bridge, pick-ups and neck specially designed for seven strings.

Ibanez Universe

Ibanez is a high-quality Japanese manufacturer well known both for its Superstrat rock-oriented guitars, such as the JEM, and its jazz instruments, such as the GB-10 (George Benson model). The Ibanez Universe was designed in conjunction with Steve Vai in his quest for a seven-string guitar, and was based on his six-string Jem models. The extra string is usually tuned to a low B note. The Universe is a contemporary Superstrat. The familiar double cutaway has a sharper profile; the lower cutaway is deeper to give better access to the upper frets. The body is made of basswood, which is lightweight and has a good bass response. The scratchplate is plastic with a mirror finish.

The neck, slightly wider and thicker than the usual Ibanez necks to accommodate the extra string, is made of maple; the 24-fret rosewood fingerboard has pyramid inlays. Both fingerboard and headstock are bound, and the frets are large jumbo style.

DiMarzio pick-ups in an HSH (Humbucker-Single coil-Humbucker) configuration are selected via a five-way switch that taps the humbuckers in positions two and four. There is one master volume and one master tone control, and the output jack is recessed.

This was the guitar that started the interest in seven-string instruments. Players looking for the extended low end and heavier sound of a low B string, without losing the high E string, have made this guitar very popular.

Parker Fly

This revolutionary instrument, which fits easily into both 'great' and 'cutting-edge' categories, was first introduced in 1993. It is based on the idea that a lightweight instrument resonates better than a heavy one. The entire guitar usually weighs in at around 2.5kg (5 lb).

The ultralight Parker Fly, made of wood and synthetic materials, features piezo saddles.

It features a very thin, contoured, wooden body core for tone, with a synthetic exoskeleton for strength and stability. The core wood is usually a medium- to light-weight wood such as basswood, alder or spruce, although newer models have bowed to player demand and now incorporate mahogany or maple. The wide, flat, and relatively thin 24-fret neck is made of basswood, and the neck join is an unusual 'finger joint' that is glued in but gives a heel profile similar to that of a straight-through neck. The fingerboard is synthetic with a 65cm (25½in) scale length and a compound radius (see p35), while the frets are of stainless steel which, being harder than most string compounds (unlike nickel silver), is extremely durable.

A very thin headstock is angled in such a way that the strings run in a perfectly straight line through the nut — a Graph Tech Trem Nut made from a space-age material that is more slippery than graphite. The tuning machines are Sperzel locking tuners. This means that tuning problems are virtually eliminated, even when using the tremolo.

The Parker Fly's bridge saddles contain piezo elements, which pick up an 'acoustic' sound from the strings. This is either blended with the electromagnetic pick-up or the two sounds are fed separately to a stereo jack. The piezo system was designed by Larry Fishman of Fishman Transducers. The bridge is a floating tremolo system with a locking mechanism that allows it to operate like a fixed bridge, a lowering-only system or a full floating system offering lowering or pullback. The ability to lock the bridge in place ensures that there are none of the usual floating tremolo drawbacks. A hand-operated balance wheel easily sets the spring tension.

CUTTING-EDGE GUITARS
BARITONE GUITARS

Similar to seven-string guitars, these are a response to players who want a lower pitched, heavier sound. However, rather than adding another string, this instrument has a longer scale and uses heavier gauge strings which are tuned lower — the low string is often tuned to a B, and sometimes even an A, below a regular guitar's sixth string.

The guitar shown below is the Ibanez MMM-1, which has the following features:
* a 72cm-scale (28in) through-neck that is a three-piece laminate of mahogany and bubinga
* the body is mahogany

The Ibanez MMM-1 baritone guitar has a 28in scale length through-neck and a mahogany body. The strings load through the body.

✳ the machine heads have low string posts providing a higher tension at the nut

✳ the bridge is similar to that of a Tune-O-Matic but does not have a tailpiece; rather, the strings feed through the body

✳ factory tuning is A#-F-C#-G#-D#-A# (first to sixth string)

✳ there are two humbucking pick-ups, a three-way selector switch, and one master volume and one master tone control.

Ron Thal and his fretless Vigier Surfreter, which has an unusual metal fingerboard to ensure good sustain on the thinner strings.

FRETLESS GUITARS

This type of guitar has no frets, rather a smooth fingerboard like a violin or fretless bass, which allows unique effects and sounds. John Cale and Sterling Morrison of the Velvet Underground recorded a track in 1965 called 'Stainless Steel Gamelan' for cembalet and fretless guitar. Frank Zappa bought one in 1973 and Adrian Belew was using one with King Crimson in 1984. The list of players using fretless guitars is growing as more and more players look for a way to extend their palette of sounds and explore new techniques.

A problem with many early attempts at fretless guitars was one of sustain: the wood of traditional fretboards tends to 'drink up' the energy of the strings, particularly the unwound strings. Modern round-wound strings tend to create wear on rosewood fingerboards and squeak when sliding; on the other hand, flat-wound strings suffer from a limited treble response, and as such are not ideal for most modern playing styles. Half-wound strings are easier on a fingerboard and do not squeak, making them ideal for the fretless guitar. Harder woods such as ebony can improve the life span of fingerboards, but ebony is rare and expensive. Maple is sometimes used with very hard synthetic finishes and some custom manufacturers use carbon-fibre fretboards and other synthetics.

There are now two manufacturers making production line electric fretless guitars: Fernandes and Vigier. The Fernandes Sustainer system is featured in its fretless guitars; this uses a magnetic field to excite the strings of the guitar so they will sustain for as long as the player wants. Vigier has been making fretless guitars for 20 years. Its Excalibur Surfreter models offer excellent sustain and fretboard durability by using a metal fingerboard. These guitars are used by artists Gary Moore, Shawn Lane and Ron Thal.

THE STICK

A modern member of the guitar and bass family, the Stick has grown from the needs of advanced players who wanted to take the tapping technique further. It is

The Stick 10 is played with a tapping technique, using both hands on the neck.

a 10- or 12-string instrument played using both hands on the neck. The strings are divided into two sets (melody and bass), each played by one hand; this affords the player similar techniques to those of a keyboard — you can play your own bass accompaniment at the same time as the chord/melody! On both the melody and bass side of the Stick, the lowest strings are in the middle of the fretboard. The bass side is like an upside-down electric bass, while the melody strings are usually tuned similar to a guitar. The fingerboard is flat with 24 diamond-shaped steel frets.

The nut mechanism allows separate nut height adjustment for each string group; the bridge and tailpiece are combined into one unit which adjusts intonation and action for each individual string.

The single stereo pick-up (one channel for each set of strings) is a humbucker with adjustable pole pieces. There are two volume controls, one for each channel.

Shielding is provided by a conductive, plastic pick-up housing. MIDI-capable versions of the Stick are also available. This specific guitar has a distinctive sound, with a longer sustain than a standard guitar. It is very percussive and has very good articulation due to the tapping method of playing.

THE ZTAR

This is not really a guitar, rather a guitar-shaped MIDI controller. Instead of strings, the Ztar has switches on the neck, one for each note. This allows a guitarist to play a MIDI controller that has the same layout and tuning as a guitar, with none of the delays of guitar-to-MIDI conversion. The Ztar also has a range of optional controllers which can be used for anything from pitch bend to drumming.

The Ztar is a guitar-shaped MIDI controller, which does not suffer from the delays that a MIDI guitar system often experiences.

CHAPTER 2

The Buyer's GUIDE

This chapter will help you make educated choices when it comes to buying an electric guitar. It takes a look at the factors you need to consider as well as the different features you can expect to see. The aim is not to push you toward a particular make or style of guitar but rather to enable you to choose the instrument that best suits your needs.

ELECTRIC GUITARS FOR BEGINNERS

Ask for help

You will need as much help as you can get when you choose your first electric guitar as there are literally thousands of makes, models and options with an equally wide range of prices. Consult with your guitar teacher, your guitar-playing friends and your music store salesperson. Find out what they recommend for your purposes and why. If at all possible, take someone knowledgeable along to help you choose.

Style and influences

Bear in mind the style of music you will be playing. It's no good buying a 'shredmeister' metal machine if your primary musical influences are jazz or blues. Take a look at the players you listen to and see what they are using. Often, players will cite a particular model or type of guitar as being best for a particular style of music (e.g. hollow-body electrics for jazz

or Telecasters for country music). However, there are no rules, and the general wisdom is at best a guideline. It is your music and your sound, so you are the one who must be happy with it.

Budget

An important factor is how much money you are willing (and able) to spend on your guitar. Don't forget that part of your budget will need to go toward your amplifier as well. While you can use all of your available money to buy a better guitar and then save up to buy an amp later, the waiting period in-between can be very frustrating.

With most electric guitars you get what you pay for, so you do need to spend some money to make sure that you are getting an instrument which is playable and free from defects. There is usually a reason the really cheap guitars are that cheap. However, if you are a beginner, generally you shouldn't spend a fortune on a top-of-the line instrument. There are certain choices you will only be able to make once you have some (or lots of!) experience playing the guitar.

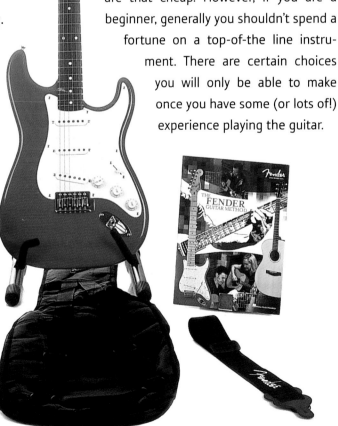

right *The contents of a 'Strat pack': this will set you up nicely with a Fender Squire Strato-caster electric guitar (featuring a double cut-away and bolt-on neck), amplifier and cable, tuner, guitar soft case, strap, and an instruction booklet.*

Take a look at name-brand entry-level instruments if you can afford them — you are assured of a certain quality and the manufacturer's backup. They may be more expensive, but when you upgrade later you will get more of your money back when you sell the guitar. Even better, some of these manufacturers have put together reasonably priced 'beginner's kits' which consist of a decent guitar and practice amp along with any number of accessories such as strap, lead, plectrum, and so on.

Keep it simple

Some features can make your early learning stages much more difficult. An example of this is floating bridges with locking nuts. While they are great for doing radical 'whammy' bar work and keeping the guitar in tune, they make changing strings and tuning difficult, especially for a beginner.

The more complex options — like multiple switches, and piezo or MIDI outputs — can be distracting; you may well spend more time fiddling around with all the options and reading instruction manuals than you do learning to play the guitar.

Use a good, basic instrument that won't distract you from learning to play — a two- or three-pick-up instrument with a fixed bridge or a non-locking tremolo. Later, when you upgrade, you will be better able to make the more complex choices.

GENERAL BUYING TIPS
Do your homework

Learn as much as you can about the myriad features available. Study the in-depth look at features appearing later in this chapter and search for user reviews on the Internet. Buy magazines to see what is available, read their reviews and get an idea of prices. The more information you can gather, the better choices you are able to make.

It's also worth speaking to other guitarists about the guitars they play; ask them why they chose their particular instrument.

New vs. secondhand

In the specific case of an entry-level electric guitar, it is advisable to buy a new guitar even if you are on a tight budget. These instruments are often not built to last, and if someone has been abusing their guitar for a year or two before you buy it, it will quite probably be a problem instrument. As a beginner, you may not have the know-how to tell if it is worth the asking price or if there is something badly wrong with it. You don't want to save some money upfront and end up having to spend a lot more than you've saved just to get it to a playable condition or to stay in tune. Buying a new instrument gives you the all-important warranty and backup from the store you bought it from.

On the other hand, if you are looking for a good instrument at a more affordable price and you know exactly what you are looking for, then secondhand is a good option. The better quality guitars have a long life span and even if there is wear or damage, they are often worth buying and repairing. Make sure you know what to look out for and how to identify problems. Also have a luthier (guitar repairman) on your speed dial so that you can get a rough estimate for repairs before you buy a damaged instrument.

Buying sight unseen is a risky proposition with a secondhand guitar unless you are buying from a known seller with a good reputation. Find out if the seller has a return policy and what it is before you buy the guitar.

Buying online

Buying a new guitar from an online store has the advantage of being cheaper than getting the same instrument from your local music store. However, this does require that you know exactly what you want. Guitars are very individualistic instruments and even with modern mass production techniques, two guitars made from the same batch of wood may sound startlingly different. There is no replacement for sitting down with a guitar and trying it out, so it's maybe not the best choice for that once-in-a-lifetime instrument.

Buying vintage & collectable guitars

It is advisable to always work through a known dealer who specializes in these instruments. As a result of the extremely high prices of some vintage guitars, it has become increasingly common for talented fraudsters to fake these instruments. Some luthiers also have the ability to repair damaged vintage instruments so that it is extremely difficult to tell that repairs have been done, which raises the value.

Most reputable dealers will be able to certify the authenticity of a vintage guitar.

Guitar customization

At one time it was very difficult to get spare parts for electric guitars. Then, in the 1970s, a large number of guitarists wanted more powerful pick-ups to drive their valve amplifiers harder. Several pick-up makers appeared to fill their need and soon other manufacturers realized the potential. Now there are pick-ups available that cover every possible sound and playing style, and a wide range of parts — even necks and bodies — to fit any guitar can be easily obtained.

DIY GUITARS

This has grown out of the guitar customization business. Once all the parts became readily available, it wasn't long before people started to assemble their own guitars. With all the hard work like neck manufacturing already done, all that's needed is enough knowledge to paint, then assemble the parts, and finally set up the guitar. International companies such as Stewart Macdonald's and Warmoth

now sell a huge range of high-quality parts and even complete kits. Warmoth also supplies the parts finished if needed, so the guitar builder only needs to assemble them and set them up.

Custom-built guitars

There are many luthiers who will build a guitar for you from scratch. This has the obvious advantage of allowing you to choose exactly what features you want in your dream guitar and having it made by a master craftsman. It is, however, usually an expensive option.

Having a guitar custom made for you (the one above is a custom-made Paul Reed Smith guitar) is the surest way to get the exact instrument you want.

EVALUATING A GUITAR

Here is a list of things that need to be checked on any guitar you are considering buying. While new guitars are obviously less problematic than secondhand instruments, they should also be checked. Bear in mind that many of the following problems are repairable, but you will need to decide whether the guitar is worth its base cost as well as the cost of added repairs.

The neck

It's very important to check the neck thoroughly. Any guitar with substantial neck damage should be avoided. Neck replacement on most bolt-on electric guitars is easy, but it probably won't be worth the time and extra expense to buy a guitar with a bad neck.

※ Check to make sure the neck is straight. Do this by looking down the neck from the headstock. You are looking for twists to the left or right, which indicate a neck beyond repair.

※ Check the fingerboard for excessive wear on either the frets or the wood between them. While the fretboard can be levelled and the guitar refretted, it is a professional job and you may need to factor it into the price of the guitar. Also, make sure that the frets themselves are not loose.

※ Examine the back of the neck and headstock for cracks or repair work. A well-repaired neck will not affect the playability or sound of a guitar, but it can affect the value of a collectable one. Also check where the neck joins the body to make sure the join is solid. If it is a bolt-on, see how well the neck fits in the neck pocket of the body. While it doesn't have to be a perfectly tight fit, it's a sign of a well-built guitar if it is.

※ Turn the tuners to see if they turn excessively easily or with difficulty. Also check to see if the keys move from side to side. Slacken the string and check to see if the post moves from side to side too easily. Replacing tuners is simple and relatively inexpensive, but worn tuners might be an indication of the condition of the rest of the guitar.

The body

※ Inspecting electric guitar bodies is quite easy: look for any large cracks. You may find dents, where the finish has been chipped off from knocks and bangs, and on bolt-on necks you may find small cracks in the finish near the neck pocket, but these are cosmetic.

The electronics

※ Testing the electronics is pretty simple: plug the guitar into an amp and play it. The selector and pick-ups are easy — try each position on the switch and make sure you get a different sound to the positions on either side of it. You should be able to tell if something is wrong. In most cases it is the switch, so move it around to see if it starts working. Switches, unlike pick-ups, are relatively cheap to replace.

※ Make sure the volume goes up and down without scratchiness and the tone controls work.

※ Then simply play the guitar for a while to see if anything jumps out at you. You can tell a lot about a guitar just by playing it. Don't allow yourself to be rushed by the seller.

Checking the straightness of the neck is one of the most important evaluations you can make when buying a guitar for the first time.

AN IN-DEPTH LOOK AT FEATURES
TUNING MACHINES

The tuning machines (also called tuners or machine heads) change the tension and thus the tuning of the strings. While tuning machines are mostly simple worm gears, there are variations on the way the mechanism is housed: 'open' indicates there is no housing at all, leaving the mechanism totally uncovered, and 'closed' indicates that the mechanism is hidden by a removable housing. The better electric guitar tuning machines tend to be the 'sealed' type, which cannot be opened; this keeps the mechanism safe from dust and contaminants. Some tuning machines have mechanisms to lock each string in place, eliminating the need for a few turns of the string to hold it. This enhances tuning stability as there is less string length to bind or stretch. The better tuning machines also have staggered tuners, where the posts of the tuners farther from the bridge are shorter. This has the same effect as an angled headstock, without the need for string retainers (see later).

inset *Tuning machine variations (from top to bottom): open, closed, sealed, and locking.*

HEADSTOCK

The tuning machines are arranged on the headstock most often in either a three-a-side configuration (3+3) or with all six on one side (6+0), although it is becoming increasingly common to find 4+2 or even a 5+1 configuration. The headstock may be straight or angled back (swept) — which allows the strings to wind evenly on the machine heads without string retainers, and also makes for an even pressure of the strings where they contact the nut. The angled head makes it easier, too, to adjust the truss-rod nut when it is at the top of the neck.

The shape of a headstock is more an aesthetic choice. However, the machine heads should be aligned to ensure the strings run as straight as possible through the nut to reduce the possibility of a string binding (sticking) and causing tuning problems.

top to bottom *Various tuning machine configurations: 6+0, 3+3 and 4+2.*

String retainers

Also known as 'string trees', these small M-shaped pieces of metal screw into the face of a straight headstock and serve to push the first two strings down. This ensures proper string angle over the nut and helps the strings wind correctly on the tuning machines. The string tree can cause strings to bind, but better models now either have small rollers or are made from graphite to reduce friction. They are not required on headstocks that are angled back.

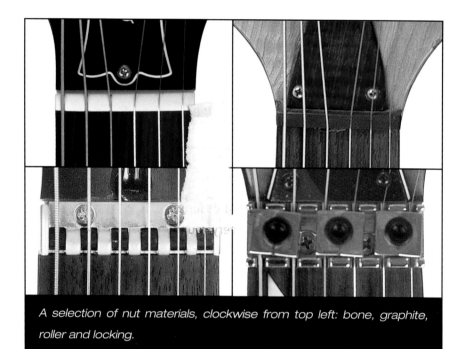

A selection of nut materials, clockwise from top left: bone, graphite, roller and locking.

Nut

The nut is what establishes both the spacing and the height of the strings above the frets. It is where the 'speaking length' of the strings' begins. Tonally, it affects mostly the open string tone.

NUT MATERIALS

Nuts are made from a variety of hard, dense materials, each having its own characteristic properties. Bone is the traditional material and, while it can be inconsistent (sometimes making one string or even one note sound different to the others), it can impart a wonderful resonance to the guitar sound. Ivory, having similar characteristics to bone, thankfully is no longer used for conservation reasons. Brass, which has a very bright tone and is very durable, was also popular at one time, but it can be hard-wearing on strings and has a tendency to bind. Synthetics such as Corian and Micarta resemble bone but are very consistent and sound good. Graphite is a self-lubricating material that prevents binding better than any traditional material, thus helping with stability and smoothness in tuning. Newer materials such as the Graph Tech polymer compounds offer even better self-lubricating properties and are also denser than graphite.

SPECIAL NUTS

Roller nuts These metal nuts use ball bearings or rollers to locate the strings and ease their movement across the nut.

Locking nuts These nuts, used with locking tremolo bridges, actually clamp the string in place, eliminating all nut- and machine-head-related tuning problems. Locking nuts do, however, necessitate fine-tuning adjustment on the bridge.

THE NECK

The neck of an electric guitar is made of harder woods to make it stable and to resist warping. It is shaped to make it comfortable for the fretting hand.

Types of wood

Guitar neck woods are hard and dense, with maple and mahogany being the two most commonly used. Maple is the traditional Fender neck wood; it has great sustain (the length of time a note will ring after being struck) and stability with a bright tone. Mahogany is not quite as dense or strong as maple, although it is very hard, and it has a warmer tone. It is the neck wood most often associated with Gibson guitars.

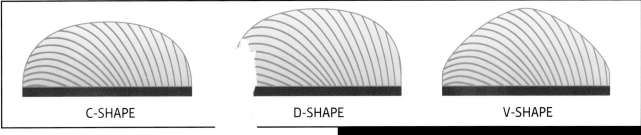

C-SHAPE · D-SHAPE · V-SHAPE

Different neck shapes and thicknesses allow for variations in tone and sustain, and also comfort.

Neck shapes

A variety of shapes and thicknesses ca⁺ ᵤersonal preference. Some guitar necks are veᵣy round, while others have more of a flattened C-shape or even a V-shape. A thicker neck will usually have a better tone and more sustain. A thinner neck is generally more comfortable, especially for players with smaller hands — although too thin a neck can be very tiring to play for any length of time.

FINGERBOARD

The fingerboard (sometimes called the fretboard) is the playing surface of a neck where the frets are located. There are two important factors: radius and type of wood.

Radius

Radius is the curve of the fingerboard across its width to accommodate the natural shape of your fingers when they are in playing position. A smaller (more curved) radius is better for playing chords, but without a high action (height of the strings in relation to frets/fingerboard), the notes will 'fret out' when you

bend the strings (buzz against the next fret or even stop ringing completely). A larger, flatter radius is better for single-note playing and bending, but is not as comfortable for playing chords. Some guitars have a compound radius, which starts out with a smaller radius at the nut and flattens into a larger radius closer to the body.

Wood

The type of wood has an impact on both the playability and sound of the guitar. Three woods are commonly used: ebony, maple and rosewood. All are dense, hard and strong.

* Ebony is a dark brown wood that's very smooth and fast-feeling, with a very bright sound and long sustain.
* Maple has lots of 'attack' and sustain, and a very bright tone — but it must have a finish to protect it, which affects the feel.
* Rosewood has a smooth feel with a warmer tone than the other two, but still has good clarity and articulation.

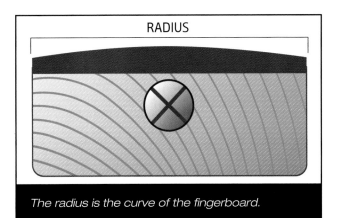

RADIUS

The radius is the curve of the fingerboard.

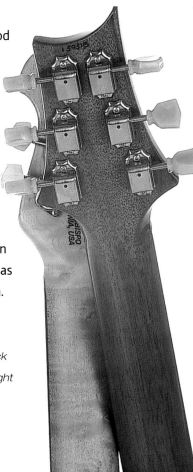

right *Guitar neck woods: the neck on the left is maple, that on the right is mahogany.*

Scalloped fingerboards

On this type of fingerboard the wood between the frets is cut away, giving it a scalloped appearance when viewed from the side. This enables a player to develop a lighter touch in fretting notes, and makes very fast, fluid runs easier. Pushing a string down toward the fretboard can be used to bend notes or even chords.

FRETS

These strips of metal run across the neck and divide the string into shorter lengths to determine a specific note when the string is pushed down (fretted). Frets are most often made from a compound called nickel-silver — actually a compound of brass and nickel. There has also been a recent trend to use steel for frets, which is harder-wearing than nickel-silver and feels smoother to play on.

A rosewood fretboard featuring narrow nickel-silver frets with abalone dots.

Height and thickness

Fret size has a great deal to do with the feel of a guitar. Low frets allow the player to feel the fingerboard but leave little room to add vibrato by pushing the strings downward, or to really grip them for bending. Tall frets are the opposite.

The width of the fret determines the amount of wear that can be expected before 'fret dressing' is necessary. Narrow frets wear faster but stay more in tune as they do, while wider frets last longer but the intonation tends to sharpen slightly as they wear.

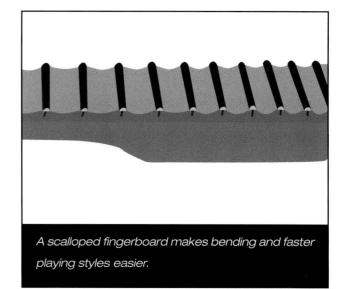

A scalloped fingerboard makes bending and faster playing styles easier.

TRUSS RODS

These adjustable steel rods are set into the neck below the fingerboard to help counter the tension of steel strings. The most common truss rod, used by both Fender and Gibson, is a single rod fixed to the neck at both ends. This design is lightweight but requires seasonal adjustment. Rickenbacker uses a double rod that is not fixed; it is extremely stable, needs no seasonal adjustments and improves sustain and tone. However, it is heavy and requires more force to adjust it.

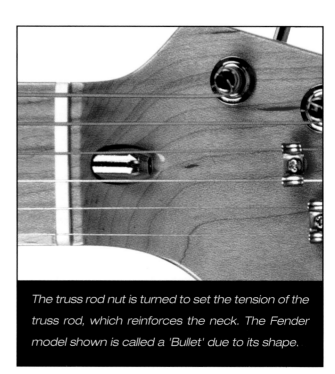

The truss rod nut is turned to set the tension of the truss rod, which reinforces the neck. The Fender model shown is called a 'Bullet' due to its shape.

NECK JOINT

The method used to join an electric guitar neck to its body can have a surprisingly large effect on the sustain as well as the tone.

Bolt-on neck

Pioneered by Fender in the 1940s with its Broadcaster, the bolt-on neck is fixed to the body by means of screws. This makes manufacturing easier and cheaper, and allows replacement necks to be fitted easily. The ability to remove the bolt-on neck simplifies much maintenance and repair work, such as refretting and refinishing. This type of neck is usually thicker at the joint and heel, with less of a cutaway possible, and this makes playing access to the upper frets more difficult. Tonally, a bolt-on neck tends to have less bass response and exhibits less sustain than other joints, however it is a sound preferred by many players. Other examples of guitars with bolt-on necks are the Fender Telecaster and Fender Stratocaster.

Glue-in or set neck

This was the original method of joining the neck to the body, and is still the preferred method of many manufacturers such as Gibson and Paul Reed Smith. Here, the end of the neck is shaped exactly to fit a slot in the body, and the two are glued together permanently. This results in a very solid neck joint that does not move, and allows for a graceful shaping of the heel to make access to the upper frets easier. The glue-in neck is relatively difficult to manufacture and repair, thus expensive. Soundwise it has a better sustain, though, and usually better bass response than a bolt-on neck.

Through-neck

In this design, the neck wood continues all the way through the body, so that both ends of the string are connected to the same piece of wood. This joint allows deep cutaways, allowing excellent access to the upper frets, a longer fretboard and a very comfortable heel. As a neck joint it is very difficult and expensive to

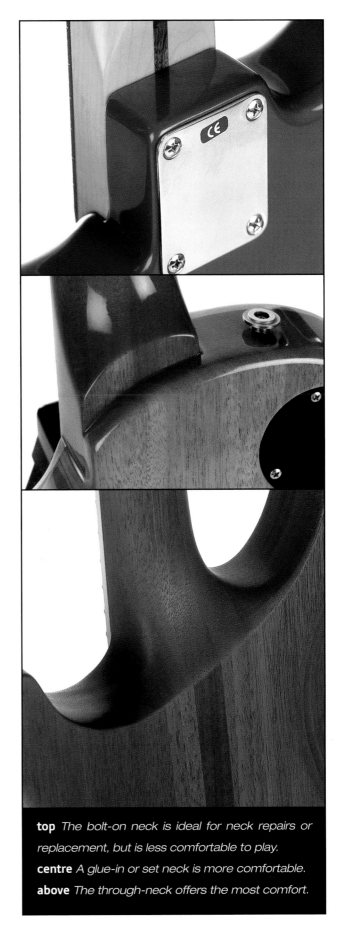

top *The bolt-on neck is ideal for neck repairs or replacement, but is less comfortable to play.*
centre *A glue-in or set neck is more comfortable.*
above *The through-neck offers the most comfort.*

manufacture; the neck cannot be removed from the guitar, making it very difficult to repair or refinish. Soundwise, through-necks have a very good bass and treble response, with excellent harmonics and sustain. Better baritone and seven-string guitars will often have a through-neck, as its extended low-frequency range and sustain is ideal for the lower notes of these instruments. Examples are the BC Rich, Jackson Soloist and Yamaha SG-2000.

SCALE LENGTH

The scale length of a guitar refers to the length of the string from where it leaves the nut to where it contacts the saddle, i.e. the 'speaking length' of the string. Two common scale lengths (usually in inches) are used on modern electric guitars: 24¾in and 25½in.

While the frequency of the notes is the same on different scale lengths, the tension of the strings will be lower on a shorter scale length. This tension difference gives a longer scale-length more attack and sustain. A shorter scale length makes it easier to bend or create vibrato notes, but is prone to fret buzz.

PICK-UPS

Pick-ups sense the mechanical vibration of the strings and convert this into electrical energy, which can then be amplified. Pick-ups for electric guitars are electro-

magnetic, using magnets surrounded by a coil of wire. They are responsible for the well-known electric guitar sound. When the guitar string moves through the magnetic field of the magnet, the variations in the field cause the coil to generate a small amount of AC (alternating current) electricity, which can be amplified by the guitar amplifier. Variations in magnet strength, shape and composition as well as number of wire windings, wire gauge and composition provide a variety of tones and power output strength.

There are two basic types of electric guitar pick-ups: single-coil and humbucker.

Single-coil pick-ups

The simplest type of pick-up, it is commonly seen on the Fender Stratocaster and similar guitars and has one wire coil surrounding the magnet structure. The single-coil pick-up generally has a more trebly sound with more 'snap' and 'punch'. It has a lower power output. It also tends to be susceptible to picking up hum from transformers and computer monitors. Another example of a single-coil pick-up is the Fender Standard.

Humbuckers

A bit more complex, the humbucker has two coils and sets of magnets in a clever arrangement that cancels out most of the hum the coils pick up. It is more powerful than a single-coil pick-up, with a smoother, bassier

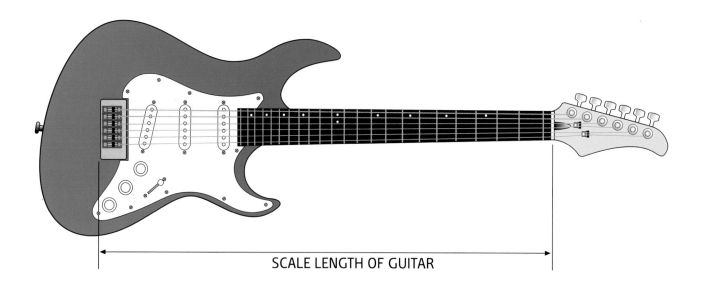

SCALE LENGTH OF GUITAR

sound. Because you have two coils and four wires to play with, humbuckers give a variety of wiring (and thus sound) options. Some of the more modern humbuckers are made full-size but are designed to sound more like single-coils. An example is the Gibson 'PAF'.

Variations on a theme

In response to guitarists who wanted to change the sound but not the look of their guitars, manufacturers came up with a number of pick-ups that look like one type but actually sound like another.

SIDE-BY-SIDE HUMBUCKERS

These humbuckers are the same size as a single coil, but they are usually more powerful than standard single coils (some are quite loud!), with more 'snap' than full-size humbuckers. Generally, the wiring options for these pick-ups tend to be as limited as a single coil, since wiring them in any other way than as series in phase gives them very thin, unusable sounds. Examples of side-by-side humbuckers are the DiMarzio FastTrack and Seymour Duncan Rails.

STACKED HUMBUCKERS

These are made to look and sound very similar to a single coil, but consist of two coils wound on the same magnets. Again, the wiring options for these pick-ups tend to be as limited as a single coil, for the reason described above.

Examples of stacked humbuckers are the DiMarzio HS and Seymour Duncan Stacks.

Pick-up configurations

The combinations of pick-ups on a guitar dictate the range of sounds available from the instrument, and a number of those available are shown on the right.

❄ Three single coils: quite flexible with a good range of five sounds.

❄ Two humbuckers: less flexible (only three basic sounds), but higher-powered sound.

❄ Two single coils, one humbucker: a flexible all-rounder.

❄ Two humbuckers, a single coil: the most flexible.

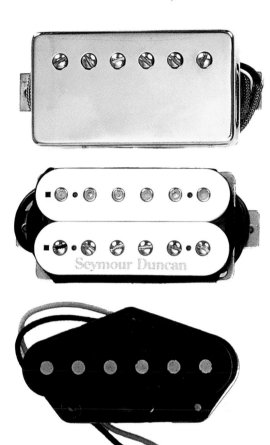
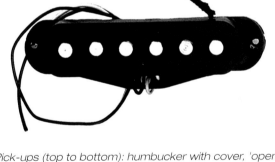

Pick-ups (top to bottom): humbucker with cover, 'open' humbucker, single-coil Telecaster bridge pick-up, single coil with cover.

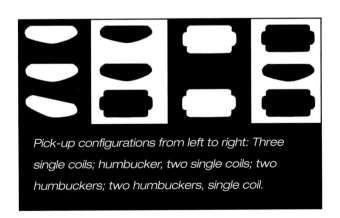

Pick-up configurations from left to right: Three single coils; humbucker, two single coils; two humbuckers; two humbuckers, single coil.

GUITAR BODY SHAPES

Body shapes are not just cosmetic; some elements of the shape will affect playability or comfort.

Cutaways

If the body is cut away where it joins the neck, this helps a musician access the upper frets of the neck. There are two types of cutaway: single, as in the Gibson Les Paul or the Fender Telecaster, and double, as in the Fender Stratocaster or the Gibson SG.

Body contour

This refers to where the guitar body is sculpted to make it fit more comfortably with the human body. A good example is a Fender Stratocaster, which is contoured at the back (called the 'tummy contour') and on the front ('forearm contour').

Balance and weight

A good body shape will be balanced weightwise, so the guitar sits well when worn with a strap without tilting toward the headstock or the body. The larger or thicker bodies, especially those made of heavier woods, can be weighty, and they can be tiring to play.

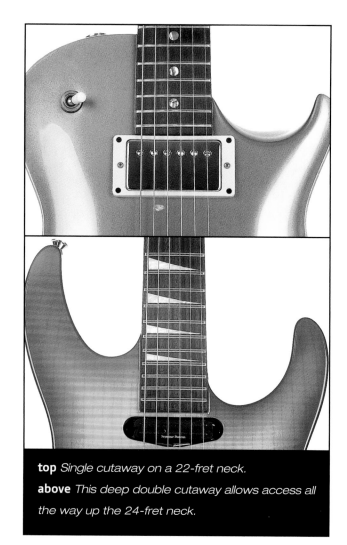

top *Single cutaway on a 22-fret neck.*
above *This deep double cutaway allows access all the way up the 24-fret neck.*

below *The contoured Stratocaster body is shaped to allow for the forearm and stomach, making it very comfortable to play.*

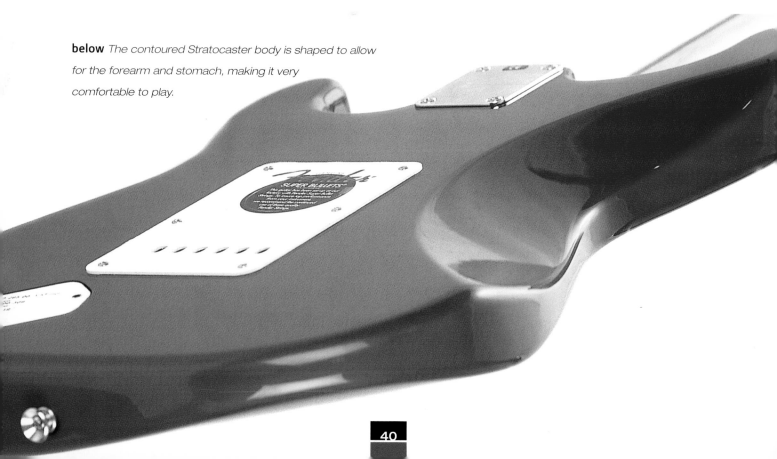

BODY WOODS

The look of each piece of wood is unique; even within one tree species, pieces vary from one to the next in grain pattern, colour, weight and density.

The sonic properties of different woods, and their different weights and densities, vary dramatically. Heavier woods sustain well and have a brighter, more articulate sound. Lightweight woods can sound indistinct or muddy, especially in guitars with humbucking pick-ups. Medium-weight woods fall in the middle and are the traditional preference. In terms of weight vs. wood types, dense woods such as maple and mahogany are heavier, while medium-density woods such as poplar, alder and ash produce a lighter guitar. Some common woods used for bodies are listed below.

❋ **Alder** has a lighter weight and a full sound. Its natural colour is light tan with little or no distinct grain lines. Alder has been the main Fender body wood for many years.

❋ **Ash** offers a very nice balance of brightness and warmth with a lot of 'pop'. It is a fairly lightweight wood with a stronger grain than alder. Many of the 1950s Fenders were made of ash.

❋ **Basswood** is a lighter-weight wood. It is white and has a warm tone.

❋ **Mahogany** is a medium- to heavy-weight wood with a fine grain. Its tone is warm and full, with good sustain.

❋ **Maple** is a very hard, heavy and dense wood. It is white and has a bright tone with good 'bite' and attack.

❋ **Flame, fiddle-back or tiger maple** has a figuring that looks like stripes.

❋ **Quilted maple** is a wood that has a billowing-cloud appearance.

❋ **Bird's-eye maple** wood has the appearance of small spots.

❋ **Poplar** has a weight and sound similar to alder.

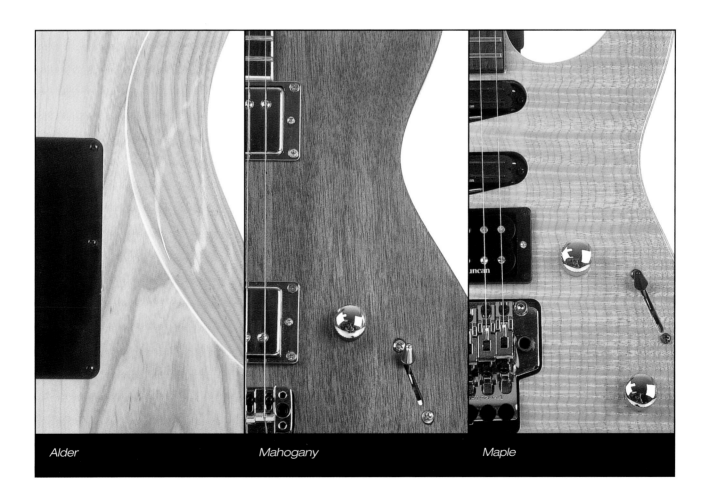

Alder   Mahogany   Maple

Finishes

Guitar finishes can be divided into four different styles.

SOLID COLOURS

These are the plain, opaque colours such as black, red or white, seen on many electric guitars. None of the wood grain shows through a solid colour.

TRANSLUCENT

These are see-through colours used when you want the wood grain to show subtly through the colour. They look best on stronger-grain woods such as ash.

clockwise, from top left *Different styles of guitar finish: translucent on alder, sunburst on alder, solid 'gold top' on maple, and dyed finish on quilted maple.*

DYED COLOURS

Here, dyes are rubbed directly onto the wood, where their absorption varies with the grain. Dyed pieces look distinctively 'alive' and have three-dimensional depth. They look best with highly figured wood such as flame or quilted maple.

SUNBURST

When the finish starts out with a light tone in the middle of the guitar body and gradually gets darker toward the edges, this is called a sunburst colour. Yellow dye is usually rubbed into the wood first, then the darker, transparent 'burst' colours are added on from the outer edges.

Binding and inlays

Originally used to cover joins in the wood as well as protect the edges of the instrument against knocks, the square edges of a guitar body, the fingerboard and sometimes the headstock are often inlaid with one or more strips of material — referred to as binding. On an electric guitar the binding will usually be plastic, although sometimes exotic materials such as mother

of pearl or abalone shell are used. Paul Reed Smith uses a distinctive 'natural wood binding' — which, although it looks like binding, is in actual fact the edge of the wood left unstained while the top is dyed.

Inlays are designs set into the wood of a guitar. These may be as simple as the dot position-markers found on most fingerboards, or complex works of art covering the entire body.

The stunning inlay work of a Paul Reed Smith Dragon is made of different kinds of shell.

BRIDGES
Fixed (non-trem) bridges

These generally have very good sustain and bass response, as there is no movement at the bridge to absorb the string vibration. This rigidity also helps with tuning stability, reducing the chance of strings binding at the bridge.

HARDTAIL BRIDGES

These are Fender-style fixed bridges — they do not move. They are screwed directly onto the body, with little to no cavity routed out below them. The strings can either pass through the body or terminate at the rear of the bridge itself.

TUNE-O-MATIC BRIDGES

This is the Gibson-style fixed bridge used with a stop tailpiece or, on older instruments, may be seen with a trapeze tailpiece. It is mounted on two thumbwheels that screw up and down into the body to set bridge height. The saddles have individual intonation adjustment, but no individual action adjustment.

STOP TAILPIECES

This is the standard Gibson-style tailpiece for solid-body guitars or those with centre blocks. It anchors` the ends of the strings in place, and is anchored to the body by means of two bolt-like posts that screw into bushings mounted in the guitar body. The strings load through the tailpiece from the back.

ARCH-TOP BRIDGES

These are designed to be held against the arch-top by the downward pressure of the strings, as most hollow-body arch-tops have no support underneath the top to screw a bridge down. They are often used with a trapeze tailpiece and come in two styles.

The first is made entirely of wood, with the top being compensated (staggered to set the intonation correctly), and is adjustable upward and downward via two thumbwheels. The second is a hybrid, which

Bridges (from top to bottom): Telecaster hardtail, Tune-O-Matic and stop tailpiece, arch-top and arch-top hybrid.

43

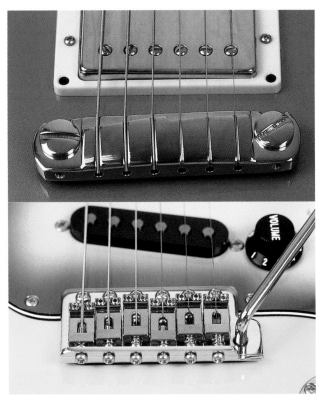

above *A six-stud tremolo (six screws at the bridge).*

top *The wraparound tailpiece serves as both bridge and tailpiece. It is a feature of many Paul Reed Smith guitars.*

left *A hinge attaches the trapeze tailpiece to the guitar.*

has the base of the wooden model, but has a Tune-O-Matic bridge on top, for adjustable intonation.

TRAPEZE TAILPIECES
Used on hollow-body arch-top guitars and some older solid-bodied instruments, these attach to the back of the guitar where the sides join. This is reinforced by a wooden block inside the guitar. The tailpiece then hinges over the top of the guitar.

WRAPAROUND TAILPIECES
A tailpiece and bridge in one, the strings load through it from the front and then wrap around the top, where they run over ridges serving as fixed saddles. The ridges are usually compensated. It can be seen on Gibson Les Paul Juniors; it is also the preferred bridge of Paul Reed Smith.

Tremolo bridges
The word tremolo, when used in reference to a bridge, is actually a misnomer. Tremolo is a pulsing variation of loudness. The effect a tremolo bridge has on the sound is actually vibrato — a controlled variation in the pitch of a note — but most people know these bridges as tremolos. They are designed to move, changing the tension and thus the pitch of the notes played.

SIX STUD 'VINTAGE-STYLE' TREMOLOS
Also called 'trems' or 'twang bars', these were originally designed to give a subtle effect, with little to no 'pullback' (raising of the pitch); the idea is that the player applies pressure to the arm attached to the bridge to lower the pitch slightly. Springs mounted in a cavity at the back of the guitar then pull the bridge back into position. Vintage-style tremolos use six

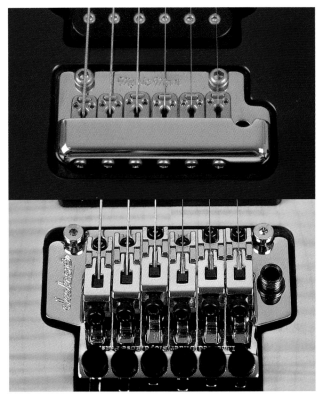

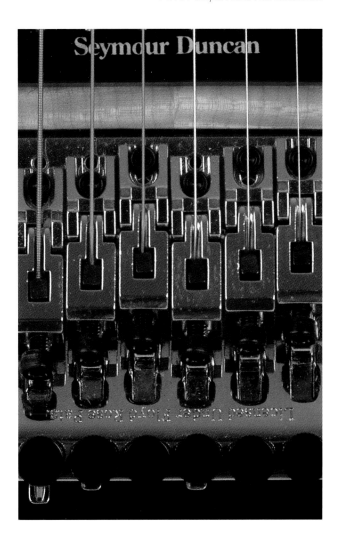

above *The locking trem, or 'floating tremolo'.*

top *A good two-stud tremolo has graphite or roller nuts.*

right *Tuning is stable with a locking trem, as the strings are clamped firmly in place at the saddle.*

screws at the front of the bridge to pivot against. They will usually make a guitar go out of tune when used aggressively, due to strings sticking at the nut, tuning machines or bridge saddles.

TWO-STUD MODERN TREMOLOS

Two-stud trems are the same as the six-stud models, but use only two studs as pivot points. They are better at staying in tune than the vintage models, especially when used with graphite or roller nuts.

LOCKING TREMOLO BRIDGES

Also called 'floating trems', 'Floyd Roses' or 'whammy bars', these lock the strings in place at the saddle so that tuning is very stable, even when used aggressively. The entire bridge balances on two pivot points, in equilibrium with the tension of both the strings and the springs in the back of the guitar. It has lots of lowering (usually enough to completely slacken the strings), and the body wood below it is usually routed away to allow enough pullback to even break a string.

A locking nut further enhances tuning stability, with tuners built into the bridge to compensate for the resulting loss of the use of tuning machines.

There are, however, some limitations. When bending a note with the left hand, the increased tension causes the bridge to pull forward, lowering the pitch of the other strings. It is more difficult to change strings as the locking nut needs to be unlocked first. Tuning up a new set of strings can also be difficult as each adjustment affects the other strings. If a string breaks while playing, the rest of the strings go out of tune, making it advisable to have a backup guitar on hand during a performance.

CONTROLS

The controls change the character of the sound coming out of the guitar. The three most common types of controls are: pick-up selector switches, volume controls and tone controls.

Pick-up selector switches

Pick-ups have a different tone depending on where they are placed along the string. The closer to the bridge a pick-up is placed, the more trebly it will sound; it has more of a bass sound the closer it is placed to the neck. Pick-up selector switches shift between different pick-ups and combinations of pick-ups to choose a variety of sounds.

On a two-pick-up guitar, a three-way switch is usually used to give the following options:

❊ Position 1 – Neck pick-up alone
❊ Position 2 – Neck and bridge pick-up together
❊ Position 3 – Bridge pick-up alone

With a three-pick-up guitar, a five-position switch is used, giving the following options:

❊ Position 1 – Neck pick-up alone
❊ Position 2 – Neck and middle pick-ups together
❊ Position 3 – Middle pick-up alone
❊ Position 4 – Middle and bridge pick-ups together
❊ Position 5 – Bridge pick-up alone

There are other options available with special switches that can, for instance, offer neck and bridge pick-ups together or even all of the pick-ups on a three-pick-up guitar. On a guitar with humbucking pick-ups, it is also possible to split the coils to offer single-coil sounds in certain switch positions.

Volume controls

These are used to vary the output level of a pick-up or even the whole guitar. Volume controls are always

Control layout on a Fender Stratocaster (although most Strats do not have the extra switch).

Other switches

There are a few other switches sometimes featured on electric guitars, which offer a wider range of sounds from the stock standard.

COIL TAPS

A coil tap switches off one coil of a humbucking pick-up, effectively turning it into a single-coil pick-up. This gives the player an authentic lower-power, single-coil sound — but does make the pick-up prone to single-coil hum.

SERIES/PARALLEL SWITCHES

A series/parallel switch changes the way the two coils of a humbucking pick-up are wired together — from the usual wiring in series to one in parallel. A humbucker wired in parallel will have less power but more treble response, similar (but not *quite* the same) to a single-coil sound — without the hum! Sometimes a miniature three-way switch is used, giving series/-parallel switching to either side of the switch and tapping the humbucker in the middle position. It is also possible (but not common) to use this switch to change the standard parallel wiring of multiple single-coil pick-ups to one in series, which gives a more powerful, thicker sound.

PHASE SWITCHES

This type of switch will reverse the polarity of a pick-up, swapping around the positive and negative outputs. While this has no effect on the sound of the pick-up by itself, when that pick-up is used together with another pick-up, all the frequencies that the two have in common cancel out, leaving only the difference between them. The resulting sound is very low-powered and has a nasal tonal character. While this sound is very interesting on its own, it is not very practical in use — tending to get lost in a mix. While it is possible to phase one of the two coils in a humbucker, the two have such a similar sound that most of the signal cancels out, leaving virtually nothing behind.

The Ibanez JEM uses a special five-way switch to coil tap the humbuckers in positions 2 and 4. This gives the guitar the much sought-after 'two single-coil sound'.

rotary potentiometers (or pots) — a type of variable resistor. As the pot is turned down (anticlockwise on a right-handed guitar, clockwise on a left-handed instrument), it introduces more resistance between the pick-ups and the output, which reduces the volume.

Tone controls

These are also always rotary potentiometers, but are wired with a capacitor that allows the pot to cut (reduce) the treble frequencies in the signal as the pot is turned down.

CHAPTER 3

Amplification

The role of the amplifier in the sound of an electric guitar should not be underestimated — it is as much part of that sound as the guitar itself.

Unlike hi-fi or PA amplification, a guitar amplifier does not strive to make the signal louder with as little coloration and as wide a frequency range as possible. In fact, it purposely limits the frequency response and dynamic range as well as distorting the signal in a multitude of ways. And it doesn't end with the amplifier. The guitar speaker does the same: it compresses the dynamic range, limits the frequency response and distorts the sound.

The Fender Cyber-Twin is a modern hybrid valve amp which features patches and MIDI control.

SOME BACKGROUND TO AMPLIFICATION

When electric guitars first started appearing in the 1930s, there were no dedicated manufacturers of instrument amplification. The only amplification available was that offered by valve (or tube) amplifiers used by the radio and hi-fi industries.

Early guitar manufacturers like Rickenbacker and Gibson would package an amp with their instruments. These first guitar amplifiers were simple copies of the same circuitry used in the original hi-fi and radio amplifiers. They usually had little to no tone modification

and the controls were on the back of the amplifier — as guitarists of the day sat behind their amplifiers.

Fender and Vox

Leo Fender started making amps in 1945 under the name K & F with his partner, Doc Kaufman. Their models had no controls at all, but relied on the guitar's volume and tone controls. In 1947 he produced his first amps under the Fender name — the Model 26 — available with 15cm (6in), 25cm (10in) or 38cm (15in) speakers.

As electric guitars became more popular in the early 1950s, guitarists started to demand more volume and flexibility from their amplifiers. Fender responded by introducing a variety of amps, from the 3½ Watt Champ to the 80 Watt Twin — all with tweed cloth covering the boxes. More importantly, he introduced more comprehensive tone circuits, with bass, middle and treble controls available on the bigger amps in the range. These highly sought-after amps are often referred to as 'Tweed' amplifiers.

In 1956 the British Vox company introduced its AC15 amplifier which, unlike everything else at the time, was designed specifically as a

The Fender Tweed Bassman is one of the most collectable vintage tube amplifiers.

left *The Vox AC-30 is one of the few guitar amps that feature a Class A design; it has a unique sound.*
below left *The Fender Blackface Twin is an amplifier that stays relatively clean at high volumes.*

needs. Of particular note is the AC30 TB (Top Boost) model, which had an extra valve and more drive than the standard model.

The early 1960s also saw Fender introduce spring reverb to his amplifiers, move the controls to the front, change the covering to black tolex (a plastic-covered cloth) and change the grille cloth to silver. The metal face-panels (where the controls were mounted) were black, which gave these amps their nickname — the 'Blackface' Fenders. (The spring reverb was a method of copying the reverb of a large room by using long springs. See also p89.)

Marshall and CBS

Also at this time, a drummer by the name of Jim Marshall, who owned a music store in London, started making amplifiers for some bass-player friends. He copied the Fender Tweed Bassman circuit and put it in a 'head' cabinet, naming it the JTM 45. To complement this, he started making various speaker cabinets, the most popular of which was the 4x12, which had four 12in (30cm) Celestion speakers in a sealed box — unlike the Fenders, which had Jensen speakers in open-backed cabinets. The Marshall cabinet gave the JTM 45 a sound that was different from the Fender

guitar amplifier. The Vox circuit was a Class A design, while every other amplifier used Class B. These amplifiers were a loud 15 watts, which distorted quite noticeably as they were turned up.

As Fender amps were rare and expensive in the UK, Vox amps were soon adopted by British bands, and the Vox sound was established. Rock'n'roll guitarists got steadily louder in the early 1960s, and Vox introduced the AC30, AC50 and AC100 amplifiers to meet their

right *The Marshall JTM 45 head, which was originally a copy of a Fender Bassman circuit.*

Bassman and, as with the Bassman, both bass players and guitarists started using them. Marshall made a few changes over the next few years, most notably to the power output valves which gave the amps the brighter, brittle tone for which Marshall amps are known. These amps also had a gold-coloured Plexiglas front panel, which gave them the nickname 'Plexi'.

In 1965 Leo Fender sold his company to CBS. The new owners changed the face plates to silver and made a number of circuit changes to 'improve' the amps by reducing distortion and making them more

The original Silverface Fender amplifiers did not sound as good as the earlier Fender designs.

In the 1970s the search for even higher gain and volume gave rise to distortion pedals and amps with extra gain stages, more sustain and more distortion — like the Mesa/Boogie amps, which were originally hot-rodded Fender models.

Marshall also came out with a master volume control in his amps, which enabled players to get more distortion, even at lower volume levels.

stable. Leo had previously resisted these changes as he felt they detracted from the sound — and he was right. As a result of bad sales of the Silverface Fenders, CBS soon changed the amps back to their original design, but by then they'd gained a bad reputation which they never escaped.

right *The Roland Jazz Chorus JC-120, loved for its clean sound, is one of the few collectable solid-state amplifiers.*
top right *The Mesa/Boogie amplifiers were originally 'hot-rodded' Fender designs, made to distort more.*

The Native Instruments Guitar Rig is a software modelling 'amplifier' which emulates a number of vintage amps and effects.

This decade also saw the advent of transistors, which enabled designers to create amplifiers that were more accurate from a hi-fi perspective. In addition, transistors operated at lower voltages and were easier and less expensive to manufacture, which led to cheaper amps. Amplifiers could be made to create a much louder effect before distorting, and they weighed a lot less. It was soon discovered, however, that valves sounded better; with valve amps, clean sounds were 'rounder' and the distortion sounds smoother and more musical. So guitarists mostly snubbed the 'better' transistor technology. Today, though, transistors (and their successors, microchips) have found their place in the inexpensive guitar-amp hierarchy.

MODERN AMPS

From the mid-1970s to the mid-1990s there were numerous small changes and improvements made to guitar amplifiers. These mostly improved control rather than tone. They included:

* rack-mountable amplifier heads and effects that bolt into 48cm (19in) rack instrument-cases
* multi-channel guitar amps, which have different preamp channels voiced specifically for certain types of sound: clean, crunch and drive
* channel switching, allowing the player to change from one channel to the next with a foot switch
* patch memories, which store the player's favourite settings and allow them to be recalled instantly
* MIDI control that lets an amp's settings be changed from a MIDI foot switch, or even a sequencer
* hybrid amplifiers that use a valve preamp (or sometimes just a single valve for distortion channel) and a solid-state power amplifier, or vice versa
* 'boutique' amplifiers — extremely high-quality updates of classic amplifiers, sometimes custom-built to order
* 'reissue' models of virtually every legendary amplifier, some made with painstaking attention to detail.

Modelling technology

In the mid-1990s Roland, a company known mostly for synthesizers, effects and other hi-tech musical items, brought out the VG-8 V-Guitar System. Utilizing any guitar fitted with a hexaphonic pickup (similar to guitar synthesizers), the VG-8 emulated a number of guitars, amplifiers, speaker cabinets, microphones and effects using 'modelling'. It could make an electric guitar sound like an acoustic guitar one second — and a Fender Stratocaster playing through a Marshall amplifier (with a Fender Bassman 4x10 cabinet) the next. Furthermore, you could put humbuckers in the Strat and mic it all with a Shure SM-57 microphone at a 15% angle, 7.5cm (3in) from the speaker — and so on.

The VG-8 emulations were good, but not perfect, so tone purists were not overly impressed — and it was a fairly expensive item. But it hinted at what was to come with modelling technology. Roland has since released its successor, the VG-88, and updated that to V2. It has also incorporated the technology into various modelling amplifiers as well as rack- and floor-mounted preamps.

In 1999 a company called Line6 came out with an amp modelling effect called the POD which used modelling technology to emulate a variety of popular amplifiers and speaker cabinets. The emulations were surprisingly good representations of recorded amp sounds, and while not perfect copies, were excellent in their own right. Since its introduction, the original POD has gone through a number of updates and improvements, and is better than ever. Line6 has also gone on to produce combination (Combo) amplifiers.

More recently, modelling technology has started appearing as computer software, using the computer's processing power for the modelling and the sound card as the guitar's input as well as the modelled amplifier's output. While there is promise for the future, the concept of computers may not yet be ready for use in a gigging environment where the requirement is for equipment that can take extreme levels of abuse.

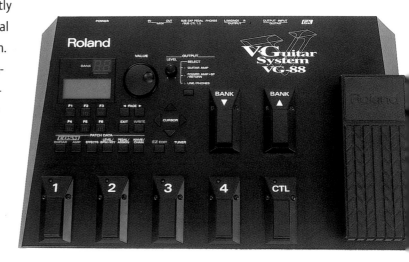

The Roland VG-88 models different guitars, pick-ups, amplifiers and microphones.

AMPLIFIER ENCLOSURES

A few different styles of enclosure are used for electric guitar amplifiers, and choice depends on your needs. If you are just practising or playing with friends, a combo makes sense. A small practice combo may not meet stadium-filling requirements, however!

Combos

Combo amps consist of a single enclosure containing both the amplifier and speakers. They range from small practice amps to large models like the Fender Twin Reverb. Combos can be quite convenient as they are usually smaller than the other systems, which makes it easier to transport them.

Stacks

When the amplifier and speakers are in separate enclosures, they are called stack systems, or stacks, because the 'head' (the amplifier) is stacked on top of the speaker cabinet(s), or cab. This style of enclosure is often used for the larger, high-powered valve amplifiers. Although large and cumbersome, they do give you the option of using different speaker-cabinet configurations. Not often mentioned, the visual aspect of playing through an amplifier stack that is bigger than you are has become standard for hard rock and metal.

above *A Marshall Twin Stack: in this system, speakers and amp (separate enclosures) are stacked one on the other.*
left *The Peavey Transformer 112 is a 'combo amp', combines speakers and amp in a single enclosure.*

Rack mounts

Rack-mounted amplifiers are made specifically to bolt into standard 48cm (19in) rack enclosures. This allows you to build a complex component system with your choice of a variety of preamps, power amplifiers and effects. Rack systems can be as small or large as required, and can mix different technologies and brands, while giving you a choice of speaker cabs.

TYPES OF GUITAR AMPLIFIER

The technologies used to create the amplifier's sound are hotly debated, with each having its proponents.

Valve (tube)

Here, valves are the key component of the signal chain. They are the heart and soul of almost every legendary guitar amp, responsible for the warm, harmonic-rich tone quality and maximum responsiveness of those amps. This is the original guitar amplifier technology, and is still the preference of tone fanatics. Valve amplifiers are much heavier, more expensive, noisier, and more prone to failure as valves are hotter and wear out. Valves must be replaced up to once a year to maintain peak performance.

Solid state

These amps use transistors or integrated circuits (ICs, chips) to modify and amplify the guitar sound. They are smaller, cheaper and more reliable, but give a harsher distortion than valves. The clean tone on solid state amps can be quite good and will usually stay clean, even at high volume levels. Jazz players often prefer solid state amplifiers over valves.

top *The Line6 POD Pro is a rack-mounting modelling preamplifier.*

centre *The Peavey Classic 5150 relies on valves for its sound – it gives a warm, harmonically rich tone.*

right *The Fender FM65R is a solid state amplifier, offering clean and distorted tones.*

Hybrids

Hybrid amplifiers use a combination of technologies, usually valve combined with solid state. Some hybrid amplifiers use a valve-based preamplifier section with a solid state power section, while others use the reverse. Some models use a single valve in the drive channel for overdrive effects.

Modelling

This is the latest technology using DSP (Digital Signal Processing) to model every element of a sound. The theory is that a guitar signal is an electronic one like any other, and valves are simply a complex form of signal processing whose characteristics and behaviour can be measured and emulated.

This is done by measuring how every part of a valve amplifier circuit responds to the signal, as well as how it reacts with other stages of the amplifier.

Also measured are elements such as how changes to the controls not only change the sounds themselves but also affect the tone-shaping properties of the other amplifier circuits. All this information is stored in a digital 'model' of the amplifier, which can then be called up to modify a guitar sound in the same way as the amplifier it is modelling.

Modelling combo amps use solid state technology for power amplification as all the tonal shaping is done in the preamp. Guitar amp modelling is still a new technology, but already it provides a very real alternative to transporting a slew of amplifiers to a gig and mic'ing them up, as long as you aren't a fanatic for absolute authentic tone and feel.

Power rating and loudness

Amplifiers are rated in watts (W), usually on the RMS (Root Mean Square) scale, which is a realistic way of comparing power ratings, unlike the meaningless 'peak' or PMPO ratings.

The relationship between watts and actual output power is an exponential one: to double the power of a 1W amplifier you need a 10W amp; to double the power again, you need a 100W model. So a 100W amp only puts out four times the power of a 1W amplifier! This also means that a stereo amp rated at 10W a channel has the same effective output power as a mono 100W model.

The relationship between power and real-world volume is an even trickier one as factors such as speaker efficiency play a large part. This is why the power ratings of an amplifier are nothing more than a general guideline, and it also explains why you will often hear someone referring to an amplifier as a 'loud 50W'. An important point is that a valve amplifier will usually have a louder perceived volume than a solid state amp of the same power rating.

In practice, a guitar amplifier rated below 20W will be fine for practising, and above that is the minimum required for band use. The power rating is a good average to go for a can be turned down in smaller venues with losing too much tone, while it can be mic'ed up and reinforced by the public address system (PA) in large settings.

left *The Roland VGA-5 models different amplifiers and speakers in a 65W combo amplifier.*

GUITAR SPEAKERS

Just like guitar amplifiers, guitar speakers are also designed to colour the sound — unlike their hi-fi counterparts. Near their maximum power rating, they limit the excursion (that is, the range of movement) of the speaker cone, creating a kind of compression. They are also built to take punishment and can exceed their maximum power ratings for short periods without self-destructing (within reason).

A hi-fi speaker and cabinet are designed to cover the entire audible spectrum (from 20Hz to 20KHz) with very little coloration (changing of the tone) and as much accuracy of detail as possible. Guitar speakers and cabinets, on the other hand, have a strong midrange emphasis.

Bass response is typically rolled off (cut off) around the low E note (82Hz) and above approximately 5KHz. Bass response is even further reduced in open-back cabinets and the midrange emphasis is a bit higher in the frequency range. They also disperse sound both forward and backward.

Closed-back, or sealed, enclosures have a tighter and punchier bass response.

Impedance

A simple explanation for impedance is: the tendency of a speaker to resist the flow of AC electricity. It is measured in ohms (Ω). At higher impedance ratings, it is harder for the electricity to get through a speaker, and at lower ratings, it is easier. A valve amplifier's output transformer is designed to work with a particular impedance or is often switchable for a number of output impedances, usually 4, 8 and 16Ω.

Using the incorrect impedance can damage the transformer, so it's imperative that the speaker impedance match that of the amp.

With solid state amplification, it is possible to use ratings higher than the rated impedance of the amp, e.g. using an 8Ω speaker on a 4Ω amp, but it will not be as loud. However, once again, if the impedance of the speaker is too low, you will damage the amp's circuitry. Most speakers used today are also rated at 4, 8, or 16Ω.

In multiple speaker setups, like many guitar cabinets, the way the speakers are connected together affects the total impedance of the cabinet. There are two ways to connect speakers together: parallel and series.

SERIES CONNECTION

In series connection, the impedance of two or more speakers is simply added together. The formula is:

$$Z_1 + Z_2 = Z_{net}$$

where Z_1 is impedance 1; Z_2 is impedance 2; Z_{net} is the resulting combined impedance.

You can add as many speakers to the left side of the equation as needed. So if we had two 4Ω speakers in series we would get:

4 + 4 = 8Ω.

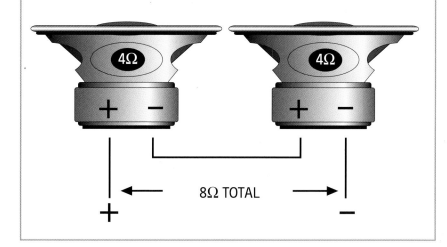

Wiring speakers in series adds the impedances together.

PARALLEL CONNECTION

With parallel connection the formula is a bit more complex:

$$\frac{1}{Z_1} + \frac{1}{Z_2} = \frac{1}{Z_{net}}$$

In the specific case of two 16Ω speakers in parallel:

$$\frac{1}{16} + \frac{1}{16} = \frac{1}{Z_{net}} \qquad \frac{2}{16} = \frac{1}{Z_{net}} \qquad \frac{1}{8} = \frac{1}{Z_{net}}$$

$$Z_{net} = 8\Omega$$

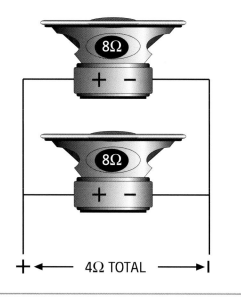

+ ◄—— 4Ω TOTAL ——►|

So, if we had an amplifier with an 8Ω output, we could use two 16Ω speakers in parallel, two 4Ω speakers in series or even one 8Ω speaker.

above *Parallel-connected speakers result in a lower total impedance.*

below *Wiring two series pairs of speakers in parallel with one another results in the same total impedance.*

SERIES/PARALLEL CONNECTION

There is another case you need to consider, that is, where you have an 8Ω amp and a cabinet with four 8Ω speakers (let's call them S1, S2, S3 and S4). While you could connect just one of the speakers to get the correct impedance, it is better to use all four speakers. So you connect S1 and S2 together in series, which gives you 16Ω. Then you connect S3 and S4 together in series for another 16Ω. Now you have two pairs of speakers at 16Ω each, so you parallel-connect the two pairs together for a grand total of 8Ω!

GUITAR AMPLIFIER FEATURES
Gain and master volume controls

Guitar amps often have a gain control (which is sometimes called 'drive', 'overdrive' or 'distortion') as well as a master volume control. This allows you to set how much overdrive you get from the preamp section, even at low volumes. Turning up the gain increases the overdrive and the master volume sets the loudness of the amplifier.

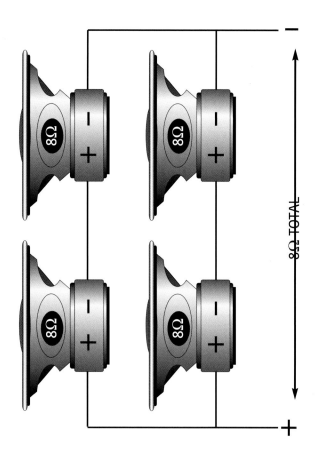

Channels and channel-switching

Many amplifiers have multiple channels, each of which is a subsection of the preamp. These channels allow a user to change from one channel to the other to get a different sound. Channels are usually voiced differently to give a different sound character and will have their own gain, volume and tone controls. There will usually be at least a 'clean' channel for clean sounds and a 'drive' channel for overdriven sounds — and tri-channel amplifiers are not uncommon.

While some older amplifiers had two channels, they required the player to unplug the cable from the one channel's input socket and plug it into the second socket in order to change from one to the other. Channel-switching allows the player to change from one channel to another without having to do this, often by using a foot switch.

Effect loops

These give you the opportunity to connect effects between the preamp and the power amp of your guitar amplifier. This is best for modulation and for time-based and pitch-based effects, as it allows them to effect the overdriven signal from the preamp as opposed to the preamp distorting the effect sounds. Compressors, distortions and so on usually work better going straight into the guitar input where they can affect the preamp gain.

Most effect loops have output jacks (called 'sends') from the preamp that run to the effects, and input jacks ('returns') that run back to the power amp. You

The Roland VGA-5 has a comprehensive array of built-in effects plus patch memory and MIDI switching.

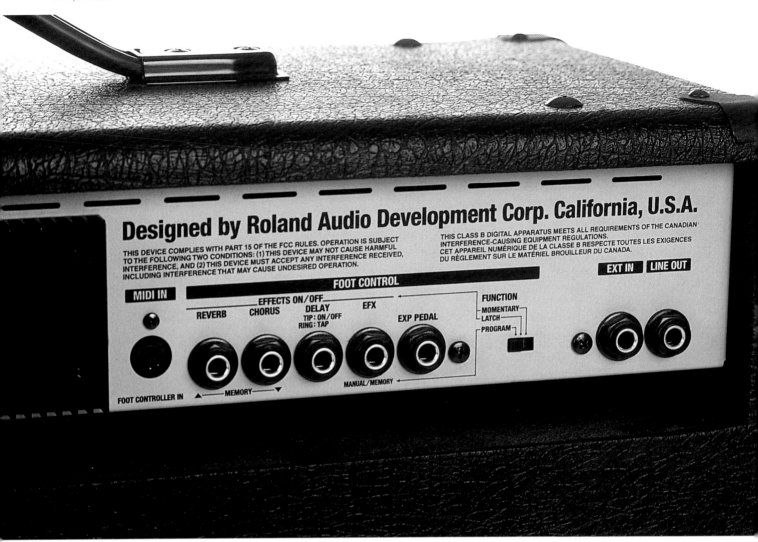

above *The back panel of the Roland VGA-5, showing the sockets for external foot controls and effects.*

may also run the preamp signal out of the send into the return of another amp to get a 'slaved' amp or simply to use one amplifier's preamp with another's power amp.

Effect sends use a line-level signal, which works better with rack-mounted effects. Some amplifiers also have instrument-level loops, which allow you to use pedal-based effects.

WARNING: Running an instrument-level pedal effect with a line-level effect send can damage your pedals! The level difference between the two is quite large.

Tone controls

Most amps have tone controls. They can range in complexity, from the single tone control of a vintage Fender to the multi-band graphic equalizers in some models of Mesa/Boogie.

Built-in effects

Most amplifiers have at least a reverb effect built in. Overdrive is also almost always built in, as it is a function of the sound of a guitar amp. Powerful multi-effect units are increasingly being built into amplifiers too, especially the modelling ones.

Proper care of valve amps

Valve amps can be almost as reliable as their solid-state counterparts if you observe a few precautions.

Buying a secondhand valve amp

✳ If you are not familiar with valve amps, take someone with you who is. At the very least, speak to a valve amp repairer beforehand, ask about the model you are going to look at and specific things to look out for with that model. Ask if it would be okay for you to phone to get rough quotes if you pick up anything untoward while you're viewing the amp.

✳ Check the speaker by giving the cone a gentle prod to make sure it's firm and not deteriorating.

✳ Turn the amp on and check to make sure there's no red-plate glow on the power valves (blue glow is OK). Don't confuse this with the normal orange glow of the valve's heater filament. A red glow indicates that the valves are underbiased, which isn't necessarily a failure but it would have to be repaired to prevent further damage.

✳ Pull all the valves and look at the valve sockets to see if any of them look cracked or burned. The seller may not let you do this, but it doesn't hurt to ask.

✳ While you are in there, look for burned or cracked resistors.

✳ Check the electrolytic capacitors for deformation or leaking. Caps do wear out and it is a common repair.

✳ Plug in and turn on. Give the amp enough time to warm up — at least 10 minutes, and preferably a half-hour. A 60-cycle hum indicates bad filter capacitors, which will need to be replaced.

✳ Listen carefully for crackles and drop-outs which might indicate bad internal components — often these don't become apparent until the amp is really warmed up.

✳ Turn on the main power switch and wait at least 30 seconds (preferably 60 seconds) before turning on the standby switch. This will help extend your valve's life span. It is also a good idea to shut off the standby switch first before turning off the mains power switch.

✳ Make sure that a speaker is always plugged into the amp before turning it on. Valve amps need to have speakers plugged in at all times.

✳ Make sure that the amp's impedance is switched to the same value as that of your speaker cabinet — you could blow the output transformer.

✳ Take a little extra care in transporting valve amps. Have a padded surface on which to put them during transportation.

✳ Make sure there is proper ventilation for the valves. Valve amps run hot — especially class A models. Don't cover the ventilation holes with anything and

also don't put the amp right against a wall so that there is no air circulating through the vents. Some players recommend keeping a fan on the amp.

✳ Change the power valves about once a year, more often if your amp is very high gain, like a Mesa/Boogie, or is used hard or every day. If you only play the amp occasionally and then at low levels, your valves should last two years or more.

✳ Do not move the amplifier immediately after shutting it off. Allow the amp to cool down for a few minutes before moving or transporting it. This helps to extend valve life.

✳ Never play on a wet or damp floor or a wet wooden stage! Some valve amps have internal voltages exceeding 600V! Never take your amplifier apart, even when turned off, as there are capacitors that store current for a long while after you have shut it off. Leave all amplifier work up to a good technician.

CHAPTER 4

Guitar ACCESSORIES

As a guitarist you will find there are lots of accessories. Some are essential items, while others are designed simply to make your life easier.

STRINGS

The sound of your electric guitar originates at the strings — they can affect tone, intonation and playability to a large degree.

STRING TYPES

The different types of string — electric, acoustic, steel and nylon — are made for completely different guitars and may not work well (or at all) on your electric guitar. Strings for electric guitar are made from various compounds of nickel and steel, which react well with the magnetic fields generated by your pick-ups. Some strings (e.g. nylon made for classical guitar) have no magnetic metals, and will not work at all on an electric guitar. Also, the plain ends of a nylon string will not attach to your electric guitar's bridge. Acoustic steel strings have the same ball end as electric strings, so these will fit on your instrument. However, the gauge (size) of acoustic strings is a lot heavier than that used on an electric guitar, and this can damage your instrument. Acoustic strings have steel core-wire and will therefore work on an electric guitar – but the windings are bronze and will not be as efficient.

Which set?

The string set that's right for your electrical guitar is a matter of personal preference. Different sets can bring out a completely different tonal character in your instrument, and even affect your playing. You need to experiment with different gauges, compounds and manufacturing methods to determine what you like best. Start with a 10—46 (light gauge) round-wound nickel-steel set; they are great all-rounders and are a good starting point. Try heavier gauges (11—48 and up) for more tone and sustain, and lighter gauges for a softer feel. Once you have a gauge you like, you can experiment with different compounds.

above *Just a few of the many types of strings available.*
below *(from left to right) The ball end of a plain string and a wound string, and a wound string showing its core.*

String construction

The thinner, plain (or unwound) strings are solid Swedish steel. The thicker, wound strings use a core wire that is usually hexagonal in shape. A layer of wire (the winding) is wound tightly around the core. The winding makes up the thickness of the string so it can produce lower notes while retaining flexibility. The end of the string has a ring of brass or other metal (the ball end) around which the core wire is wrapped; it serves to fix the string in place at the bridge of the guitar.

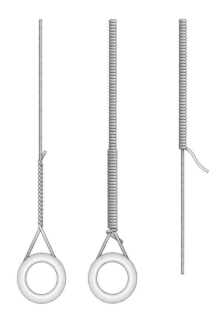

Electric string compounds

Pure nickel Most strings used in the 1950s were wound with an alloy called pure nickel. Recently they have become popular again with players looking for a retro tone. They are warmer sounding than nickel-plated ones; their smoother feel is better suited to jazz and blues. Not being as magnetically effective as steel, their volume output is lower than nickel-plated strings.

Nickel-plated Most wound electric strings are made of a steel alloy with pure nickel plating. The sound of an unplated steel alloy is too bright for some players, and nickel plating warms up the sound and improves oxidization resistance. It also provides some surface softness, which reduces finger 'squeak' and fret wear.

Stainless steel With their excellent magnetic properties, stainless-steel strings have exceptional brightness, volume and sustain. They are very durable and don't tarnish or corrode. Stainless steel has a different feel to nickel-plated strings, and being a harder material than the usual nickel-silver frets, causes more fret wear. Its bright sound may be a little too harsh for some players but it is becoming quite popular with others.

Gold-plated Gold plating on a string softens the tone very slightly, but makes the string last a lot longer due to its corrosion resistance; it also has excellent hypo-allergenic properties.

Polymer coating This modern 'plastic' coating makes strings completely corrosion-resistant. These strings retain their 'new' sound for a very long time and are extremely durable. With thicker coatings they have a softer sound and reduce finger 'squeak'.

Winding types

ROUND-WOUND

Strings using round wire for the winding are the most common. They produce a bright, clear sound with good sustain.

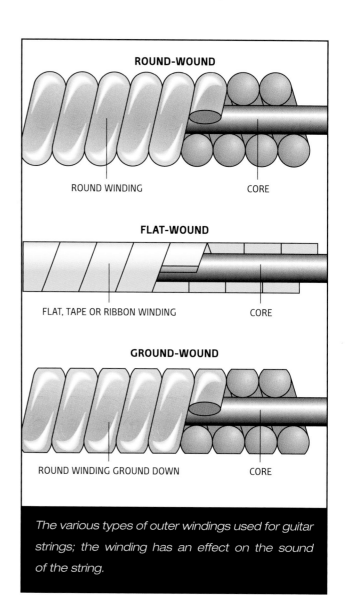

The various types of outer windings used for guitar strings; the winding has an effect on the sound of the string.

FLAT-WOUND (TAPE-WOUND)

Flat- or tape-wound strings are wound with a flat, ribbon-like wire that produces a smooth outer wrap. This provides for easy sliding and eliminates finger 'squeak'. They have a mellow, full sound that emphasizes the fundamental at the expense of harmonic overtones and sustain. They are typically used by jazz players on hollow-body arch-tops.

GROUND-WOUND (HALF-WOUND)

These round-wound strings are ground or polished to leave the outer surface of the string smoother, but not completely flat. In terms of finger 'squeak' and tone they fall between round- and flat-wound strings.

PLAIN STRINGS

These strings are made from Swedish steel. Most lighter electric sets use plain string for the first three strings; the heavier sets may use them for the first two. Plain strings have excellent magnetic properties and sustain.

String gauge and tension

Sets of strings are gauged so that with standard guitar tuning they feel similar in tension. However, it is not the gauge that is important but the mass of the string. As the gauge increases, so does the mass, but two strings of the same gauge will not necessarily have the same mass. The metals used, the size and type of core wire, and the size and type of wrap wire could all be different. Nearly all plain strings, regardless of brand, are made of similar steel, so have the same density and a similar tension for the same gauge.

Higher-tension strings (harder to play as a beginner) will sound louder. As they vibrate over a smaller area, you can normally achieve a lower action without fret buzz.

Punishing playing styles, such as the one Jimi Hendrix was known for, wear out strings very quickly.

They produce purer tones with better articulation and allow faster picking. Lower-tension strings allow easier string bending and have a softer action and sound.

STRING WINDERS

Also known as peg winders, these labour-saving wonders are simple devices that let you turn the tuning machines quickly and easily when winding on new strings. They are one of those items you think you can do without, until you have one — then you wonder how you ever coped without it. They are really inexpensive, so there's no excuse not to own one.

I have seen electric models, something like a cordless screwdriver but, personally, I prefer to feel the tension of the strings as I turn. After a while you get to know almost exactly how much to turn the key so the string is nearly at the correct pitch, simply by feeling the tension as you wind.

PLECTRUMS

Sometimes called picks, these are often an overlooked aspect of playability and tone. Plectrums (sometimes referred to as plectra) come in a variety of shapes, sizes, colours, materials and thicknesses — all with their own feel and sound. Many well-known players will tell you that a huge part of their sound is due to the plectrum they use.

Presented here are just a few of the scores of plectrums available. The shape, materials used, thickness and size all play a role in the sound produced.

SHAPE

There are differences in sound due to factors such as thickness, edge bevel and flexibility. Generally speaking, a sharp-tipped, thin plectrum will have a bright, quick attack with a fair amount of percussive 'click'. On the other end of the spectrum, a thick (say 1.5mm), round-cornered plectrum will have a very broad, warm tone with a less pronounced attack and less plectrum noise on the string. Some popular plectrums have different edges that let you obtain a range of sounds.

SURFACE

Many companies offer different grips (from matt surfaces or raised lettering to perforations) which make it easier to hold on when your hands start to sweat. A rough surface at the edges of your plectrum will give a more percussive sound.

PICK MATERIALS

Plastic The most common plectrums these days are made of various types of plastic: nylon, delrin and tortex are three of the most common.

Celluloid The world's first plastic, this was at one time the only material for plectrums. Some vintage buffs still prefer the sound and feel. The erratic and flammable nature of celluloid has led to its being replaced by other more stable plastics.

Tortoiseshell This used to be a quite common material but since a ban on its manufacture and distribution in the mid-1970s, these plectrums are virtually impossible to locate. They were very stiff, very durable and had a rich complex tone. They were also quite easy to reshape by sanding and filing.

Metal Some players prefer the brash, bright sound of metal plectrums. They can be made of copper, stainless steel, aluminium – even a copper coin can be used (both Brian May and Billy Gibbons swear by coins!).

Other materials Stone, felt, wood, graphite and other more exotic materials have been used to make plectrums, but tend to be rare.

THE RIGHT ONE FOR YOU?

The key to finding the right plectrum is experimentation. Sometimes different styles of playing require a different plectrum. So it's good to keep an open mind and have lots of different plectrums on hand.

STRAPS

Straps hold your guitar in the playing position, even when you're standing. They also prevent your prized instrument from crashing to the floor. For these two reasons alone they are worth the relatively low price of purchase. Electric guitars are actually designed to balance best when supported by a strap. This allows a more natural hand position and does away with the need to support any of the weight of the guitar with the left hand. A good, wide strap will distribute the weight of your guitar over a broad area of your back and shoulders, reducing fatigue and preventing you from developing back problems.

Electric guitars carry special strap buttons at the base of the body as well as on the top cutaway or the area where the neck is joined to the guitar's body. Strap ends feature a keyhole-shaped slot that fits over these buttons. Any standard strap fits the buttons.

Straps come in a variety of materials, widths and colours and are usually length-adjustable to allow for player preference. Leather and cloth are popular as materials; so are synthetics such as nylon.

A variety of manufacturers make strap locks — mechanisms that remove any possibility of a strap coming loose from the strap button and falling. They are always worth having, especially in an energetic playing situation or where the guitar is played in a very low-slung position, with the neck tilted upward at an angle.

When playing a low-slung guitar like Jimmy Page of Led Zeppelin, it's easy for the strap to come loose unless strap locks are used.

CASES AND GIG BAGS

Guitar cases and bags are essential investments as they protect your guitar during transport or storage, greatly reducing the chance of any damage. A variety of types is available, offering varying degrees of protection. Hard cases usually have a lock for extra security during transport — but this doesn't prevent the entire case and contents from being stolen!

Carry bags

These simple guitar-shaped covers, often with shoulder straps but no padding, are inexpensive and the shoulder strap makes carrying the guitar very conven- ient. They offer only a small amount of protection against scratches, however, and no protection against knocks.

Gig bags

These are padded carry bags with the same advantages, but offering better protec- tion against bumps and scratches.

Hard-foam cases

These cases are blocks of hard foam covered with woven nylon. They are not as strong or rigid as hard-shell cases but offer a lot of padding and are lightweight. They protect very well against knocks and scrapes, but due to the flexibility of the foam do not protect from heavy weights.

Hard-shell cases

Standard hard-shell cases are made of moulded ply- wood or superwood (compressed wood/hardboard) and covered with vinyl, which holds the case together. They come in shaped or rectangular varieties. The only difference between the two is that a rectangular case has more storage space inside for accessories and is

slightly more awkward to carry around. Hard-shell cases offer protection against knocks and scratches during transport and are fairly durable and splash- proof. However, the wood can be damaged or mis- shapen by excesses of water, and

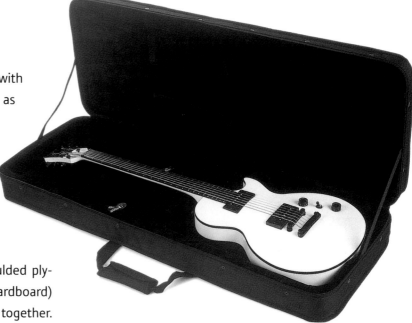

above *Hard-foam cases are well padded but are not rigid.*
centre *Padded gig bags will protect against scratches.*
top *Carry bags unfortunately offer very little protection.*

above *Flight cases offer the best protection but are heavy.*

centre *Moulded cases are light and waterproof.*

top *As a protective case, hard-shells are fairly durable.*

once the vinyl is badly worn at the seams, these cases have a tendency to fall apart.

Moulded cases

Made from injection-moulded rigid plastics, and usually with an aluminium trim, these cases are very strong, light and often completely waterproof. They offer excellent protection against knocks, scratches and moisture. Their only weakness is that they warp in extreme heat; however, these are the same extreme temperatures that will destroy an electric guitar, regardless of its case. They are more expensive than the standard hard-shell case, but are more durable and impact-resistant.

Moulded-case manufacturers sometimes make a moulded case within which the first case is stored. This adds an extra layer of protection to the instrument and makes it nearly as safe but still a lot lighter than a flight case.

Flight cases

These are designed with professional road use in mind, where they may need to protect guitars from heavy items such as a rack of amplifiers falling onto them! They may be made from thick wood with an additional waterproof covering, fibreglass, aluminium — or, for the paranoid instrument owner, even carbon fibre! Most flight cases are rectangular or trapezoidal in shape. They are bulky and heavy and can cost several times as much as a standard hard-shell case, but they offer the ultimate in protection.

Case covers

While it may seem strange to have a cover to shield the case that's protecting your guitar, this relatively inexpensive item does extend the life of a hard-shell case many times over. Gibson instruments were issued standard with case covers in the 1930s, and often still come with the pristine, original cases.

ELECTRONIC TUNERS

These help you to tune the guitar so it's in tune with itself and other instruments. The tuner detects the note being played on the guitar and displays a visual indicator that shows whether you should tune the string higher or lower. Electronic tuners are very simple to use, especially for beginners who might not have developed pitch recognition skills, enabling them to tune the guitar to a specific note from another instrument, pitch pipe or tuning fork. Tuners come in two varieties: the six-note tuner and the chromatic tuner.

Six-note tuner This allows you to tune the six strings of the guitar to standard pitch. Usually, you select the individual string you want to tune by setting a switch.

Chromatic tuners You can tune to any note in the chromatic scale (all 12 notes), not just the six in standard guitar tuning — and it allows you to tune other instruments in addition to your own guitar.

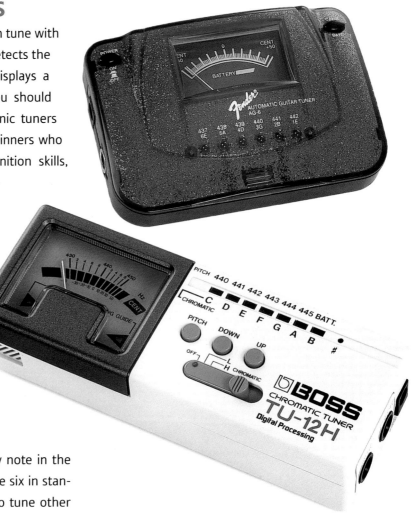

above *Chromatic tuner: allows tuning to any note or pitch.*

top *Six-note tuners: for tuning a guitar to standard pitch.*

ELECTRONIC TUNER FEATURES
Meters

VU meter Uses a needle indicator; it is easy to use and accurate, but not that visible on a darkened stage or from a distance, even when backlit.

LCDs (Liquid Crystal Display) Sometimes used in place of VU meters, but they are not practical in this application as they also need to be backlit and are often not visible from an angle.

LEDs (Light Emitting Diodes) These are the small red lights you see on many electronic devices. They are easily visible from a distance or in low light. However, these are usually not as accurate as VU meters.

Ideally, your tuner should have VU meters and at least two LEDs (arrows, telling you to tune up or down).

Input jack

This allows you to plug an electric guitar directly into the tuner, which is more reliable than using a microphone, especially in a band situation where a mic will pick up other instruments.

Output jack

This allows you to leave your guitar plugged into the tuner while using another cable from this jack to your amp or effects pedals.

Microphone

If the tuner has an input jack, your electric guitar will have no specific use for a microphone, but it does come in handy for tuning acoustic instruments that have no pick-up.

Hands-free operation

This means you can simply play the string/note you want to tune and the tuner automatically identifies that note. It does away with the need to set a switch for each string you tune, thus speeding up the tuning process.

Battery operation

Virtually all electronic tuners use a battery for portability. It is worth mentioning that you should always use alkaline batteries for tuners and other electronic devices, as they are less prone to leaking than the regular zinc-carbon batteries. Even if they do leak, the contents crystallize on contact with air, usually before doing any damage.

Power jack

This enables you to use a power adaptor to supply the tuner, which saves on the cost of batteries (although most tuners will run for a very long time on a single battery). The power jack is especially useful if you incorporate the tuner into a pedal board that uses a single power supply for all your stomp box effects.

CABLES

A guitar cable connects an electric guitar to an amplifier. Due to the low current and high impedance signal from an electric guitar, it is quite a critical item in the signal chain. Ideally, a guitar cable should not change the sound produced by the guitar or pro-

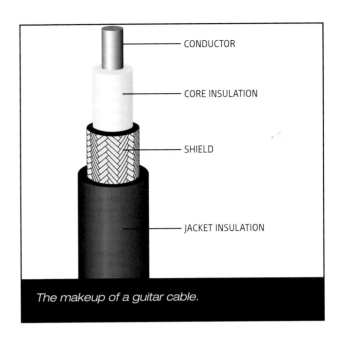

The makeup of a guitar cable.

- CONDUCTOR
- CORE INSULATION
- SHIELD
- JACKET INSULATION

duce any noise when moved, and should also stop interference from affecting the signal. It should be able to withstand the rigours of gigging by performing despite abuse — and it should remain flexible, too!

CONSTRUCTION

Guitar cables are constructed using single-conductor audio cable with an overall shield, terminated in 6.35mm ($\frac{1}{4}$in) 'phone' plugs.

Plugs

These standard 6.35mm ($\frac{1}{4}$in) phone plugs come in two basic styles: straight and angled. The straight plug is most common and is what you need for most guitars. An angled plug has the shaft coming out of the plug casing at a right angle to the cable, and is used when the output jack is on the face of your guitar. It can't be used with the angled jack socket of a Stratocaster type instrument, though.

left *A range of 6.35mm ($\frac{1}{4}$in) jack (phone) plugs.*

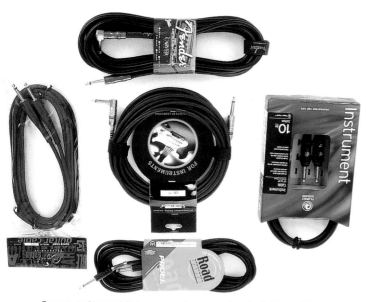

Some guitar cables are made more for flexibility, while others are made for durability or cost effectiveness.

Cable

The cable itself consists of: a core conductor wire that carries the signal; a core insulator that stops the core and screen from connecting and 'shorting out'; a screen (shielding) wire that intercepts interference and drains it to earth; and an outer insulation or 'jacket' that protects the cable and is usually made of rubber.

THINGS TO LOOK AT
Plugs

Must be solidly constructed and offer some kind of support (called 'strain relief') where the lead leaves the casing. When buying cables, it is a good idea to unscrew the cover of the plugs to make sure that the plug is solidly made and that any soldering is solid, neat and shiny. If the solder is dark grey or has excess whitish corrosion, then it probably hasn't been well soldered. Do not use plastic plugs, as they offer no shielding against interference; one-piece moulded plugs are a sure indicator of a cheap (and noisy!) cable.

Cable thickness

The first thing to look out for is the thickness, as thin cable either has less actual wire in it or less insulation

— or both. Too little wire and the resistance will be higher, blocking the signal from the guitar; too little jacket insulation and the cable will not have adequate protection from abuse.

Cable length

Use a cable that's only as long as you need; if it's too long, it will have high resistance and be more prone to picking up interference. An ideal length is approximately 3m (10ft), while the longest cable run recommended is 9m (30ft).

Flexibility

Find a cable that's flexible. Stiff cables don't lie flat on the floor and are prone to permanent twisting.

Shielding

Braided shields work better than spiral, 'wrapped' shields. The braided shield should be tightly woven, not a loose braid, to provide better screening, but will not be as flexible. Some manufacturers do use a loose braid with a layer of semi-conductive plastic to provide 100% screening while remaining flexible.

Oxygen-free cable

An OFC (oxygen free cable) lasts longer as the copper wire does not oxidize.

Sound

Avoid cables that advertise a specific 'sound', as these actually modify the signal from the guitar by filtering out some of the frequencies. Guitar cable should have a 'transparent' sound, neither adding to nor subtracting from the guitar signal.

Curly cable

These 'curly', stretchy cables used to be popular but are prone to wear due to constant stretching and contracting. They have also been known to come flying out of Stratocaster-style side-angled jack sockets when stretched too far!

OTHER ACCESSORIES
CAPOS

A capo (capodastro) is a clamp-like device that you fix to the fingerboard of the guitar between the frets to change the pitch of all six open strings. It can be thought of as an artificial barré, and this makes changing the key of a song very easy.

Each fret on the guitar is a half-step in tone, so if you put a capo on the first fret, all of the open strings will sound a half-step higher in tone than normal. Place the capo on the second fret and the open strings will all sound a whole tone higher.

For example, if you have a song in the key of G with the chords G, C, and D, you could change the song into the key of A without having to relearn it. You would simply put a capo on the second fret, and play the chord shapes G, C, and D; they will sound a whole tone higher as per the chords A, D and E.

A good capo should hold down all the strings with even pressure. If the pressure is too light, the strings will not push down to the frets properly and the string will buzz. If the pressure is too high, it will bend the strings slightly and make the notes sharpen in pitch, affecting the tuning. When putting a capo on, make sure it's close to the fret; this lessens the chance of strings bending out of tune.

There is a wide variety of makes and models of capos available. The best way to choose one is to try it and see if it works for your guitar and playing style. Capos made of metal are usually more durable than those made of plastics and elastic.

Shape

Capos are made for flat or curved fingerboard shapes as they must clamp the strings down with roughly equal pressure. For electric guitars, whose fingerboards feature a radius (see p35), the curved models are the ones to use.

A few types of capo are self-adjusting, which will work with any radius of fingerboard, and even an electric 12-string!

Different types of capo (from top to bottom): Jim Dunlop, Heriba, Shubb, Keyser. Not shown: the inexpensive elastic capo.

Speed of use

Preferably, you want a capo that's quick and easy to engage and release. Some capos will slide up over the nut and onto the head-stock, ready to be brought into use quickly. Make sure that the capo engages and releases smoothly. This usually indicates that the mechanism is of a better quality and will be durable.

Wall hangers keep a guitar out of harm's way.

GUITAR STANDS

These allow you to stand your guitar up and hold it securely so it doesn't fall over. It is an essential item for the gigging guitarist, as the common practice of leaning a guitar against an amp is probably the leading cause of broken guitar necks. A guitar on a stand is also ready for instant use. Stands should be sturdy and have padding where they support the neck. If you have an instru-

left *Single floor stand with neck support.*
centre *Floor stand for multiple guitars.*
right *Single floor stand that does not offer neck support.*

ment with an unusual shape, the stand will need to be adjustable to accommodate it. It is best to place your stand next to your amp with no space to walk in-between; this ensures that no-one trips over the cable and launches your guitar across the stage.

At home or in your studio, wall hooks on which to hang your guitar are ideal: the guitar is ready for use, and out of the way of vacuum cleaners, toddlers and pets. Make sure the hooks are properly secured; it defeats the purpose if they're insecurely mounted.

METRONOMES

A metronome is a device that maintains a steady tick or beat during practice to improve your timing and tempo. It measures time in beats per minute (bpm), so 60bpm means one beat a second.

Ideally, a metronome should also be able to accent the first beat in different time signatures. The audible accent will help you to stay in time.

Traditionally, metronomes were clock devices that used the soundboard of a piano to amplify the ticking they create. For electric guitarists, electronic metronomes are more suitable – they can be louder, especially models with an output jack to plug into an external amplifier. Another option is to use an electronic drum machine as a metronome, as it can be used both to supply a simple click or to play more complex drum rhythms, so you can practise working with different rhythms too.

CARE PRODUCTS

Guitar care products include:

Polishing cloths: high-grade, soft, lint-free cloths for cleaning and polishing your guitar. These will keep it in good shape without scratching even the most delicate vintage finish.

Polishes: to shine up your guitar.

Lemon oil: to clean and oil a fingerboard occasionally.

right *A metronome is an important practice tool.*

String cleaners: these clean and lengthen the life of your guitar strings.

String lubricants: make playing slightly easier and help reduce string 'squeak'.

above *A variety of guitar care products includes: string cleaners and lubricants, lemon oil, guitar polish and a soft polish cloth.*

CHAPTER 5

Electric Guitar
EFFECTS

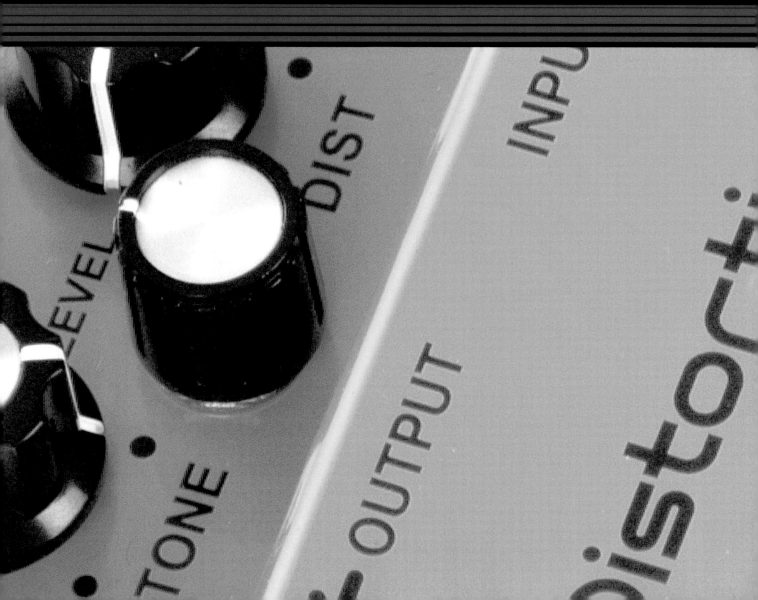

Probably the main thing to understand about guitar effects is that they modify the sound they receive. Each effect has its own particular sound — although some effects do sound similar to others. They fall into a number of broad-based categories, depending on how they achieve the sound they create. The categories are:

* EQ/tone: changes the tone of the guitar
* Modulation: applies various pulsing effects
* Level/dynamics control: affects the level of the guitar or the dynamic range (the range of volumes from quietest to loudest)
* Distortion: provides effects similar to overdriven amplifiers
* Pitch-based: changes the pitch of the instrument
* Time-based: uses time-delayed sounds

POWER REQUIREMENTS

Most pedal-type effects use 9V batteries or can be supplied by a 9V power adaptor.

Batteries

If you have only one or two pedals, the use of batteries will simplify matters. There are less wires to trip over than if you have a power adaptor and its lead. Certain types of effect, such as overdrive, can last for months on a single battery, making this an economic proposition. Make sure you use the more expensive alkaline batteries, as they are not only more cost effective and longer lasting, they also rarely leak. If by some chance they do, there will be little to no damage.

Power adaptors

For those with a wide array of pedals, it can prove to be expensive to make use of batteries. Also, certain pedals such as digital delays and reverbs can be extremely power-hungry, draining an alkaline battery in a matter of hours. These are prime candidates for power adaptors. They come in a variety of power ratings, from the smaller ones that can supply only one effect to more powerful models that will run 10 or more pedals with no difficulty.

To select an adaptor that has enough power to run all your effects, check each effect's current rating, which is rated in milliamps (mA; 1000mA = 1 amp), then add all of these figures together. The resulting figure is the minimum power rating you should use. It's safe to purchase an adaptor that's rated higher than your needs, as long as the voltage is the correct voltage (usually 9V).

Your power adaptor may have only one plug for effects. To use it with more plugs, buy a daisy chain power lead, which takes the plug from your adaptor and splits off into four or five plugs for multiple units. For the more intense applications where you have a lot of effects, you would ideally also choose an adaptor that has a separate power output for each pedal you use. This avoids the occurrence of earth loops (see below), which can create large amounts of hum.

Earth loops

Occasionally you might find that when you combine two effects and use a single power adaptor for both,

above *A power adaptor will save you money on expensive batteries, especially where power-hungry digital pedals are concerned.*

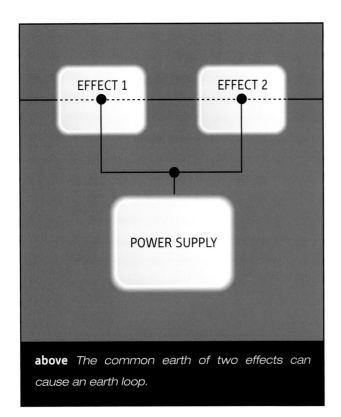

above *The common earth of two effects can cause an earth loop.*

you get an extremely loud hum. This is usually caused by an earth loop. This is where the earth connection of the signal between the two effects and the shared power rail creates a loop that acts as an antenna, picking up excessive hum. While some people would recommend breaking the earth connection in one of the leads to break the loop, it's better to use either a dedicated power supply for one of the pedals or a specialized power supply with multiple power circuits.

EFFECT PLACEMENT

In a chain of effects (often called the signal chain), there is often a particular order that works best, or is most commonly used (see illustrations opposite and p80, followed by effect descriptions).

However, this is not set in stone and it pays to experiment with the order of your pedals. Swap them around to see what the results are and what works for

right *A suggested way of ordering effects in a chain; it is not the only option.*

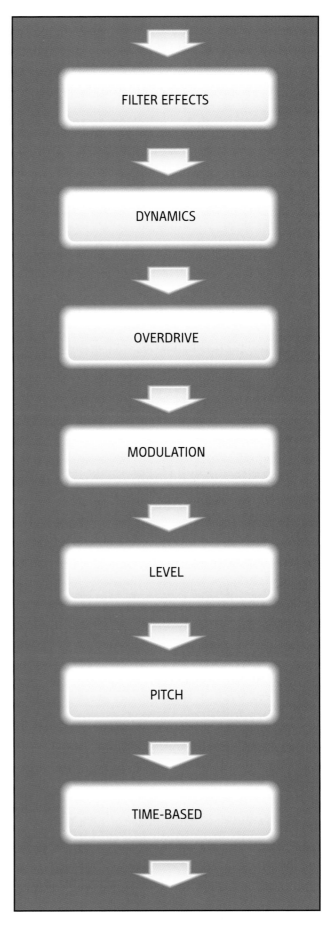

FILTER EFFECTS

DYNAMICS

OVERDRIVE

MODULATION

LEVEL

PITCH

TIME-BASED

you. The more you learn about the sounds they create and how they react with each other, the easier it will be to create your own sounds.

LEVEL MATCHING

When using more than one effect, it's advisable to practise level matching. This is where, by setting the level control, you ensure that the level coming out of an effect is roughly similar to the level of the input. This practice makes sure you don't overload the input of the next effect in line and cause undesirable distortion. It also ensures that you get the lowest noise from each of the effects.

To set the level of an effect, bypass it and play a sustained note or chord. Listen to the level and turn on the effect while the sound is still sustaining, then listen for a level drop or boost. Set the level so they match, then check again. Once they are the same, move on to the next effect in the chain.

PEDALS VS. RACK UNITS

Compact pedals are designed specifically for guitarists. They are made to go in-between the guitar and the amplifier, which is a relatively low signal level. They are unfortunately not suitable for use in an amplifier's effect loop or with other line-level signals.

Rack-mount effects are larger and designed to bolt into the standard 19in racks. They are usually of a higher quality and have more options and controls than pedal effects.

Originally used by recording studios and sound reinforcement companies, it didn't take long for guitarists to start adopting these powerhouses and to build their own rack systems to take on the road so they could access the additional power and sound quality they were accustomed to using in the studio.

left *Standard-size racks afford guitarists great versatility and convenience in terms of the multiple effects they hold.*

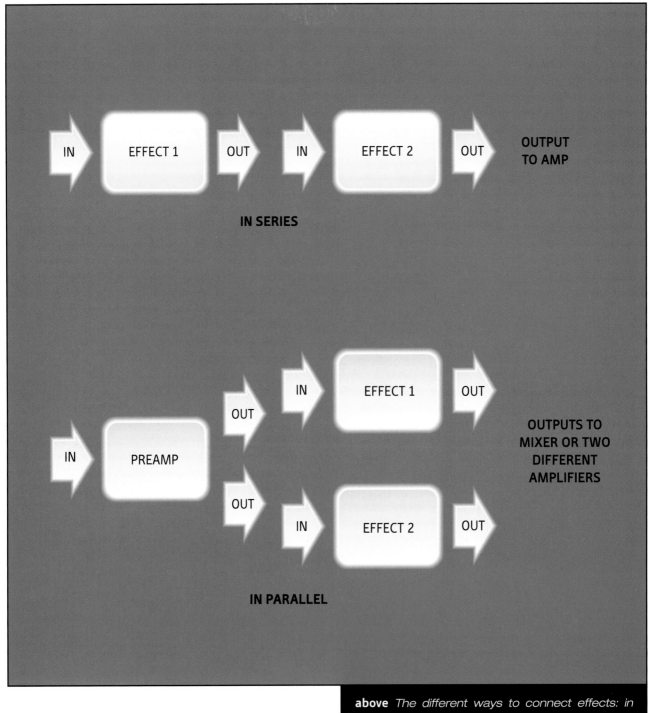

IN SERIES

IN PARALLEL

Using effects in series or parallel

The most common way to connect effects is in series, where the output of one effect feeds the input of the next. There is another, less often used option, which is to connect them in parallel. Here, the signal is buffered (powered by a preamp), and is then used to drive both effect inputs. The two effect outputs are then either mixed together or each is taken to a separate amplifier. This means that a wide array of 'blended' sounds can be obtained, e.g. an overdriven sound mixed with a clean, chorused sound instead of an overdriven chorus sound or a chorused distortion.

THE DIFFERENT EFFECTS

WAH PEDALS

Type: EQ/tone

The wah pedal produces a very expressive effect that matches the vocal 'waa' sound. It is usually controlled manually by the foot, moving a rocker pedal, similar to a volume pedal. A wah creates a 'peak' in the frequency spectrum (by boosting a narrow range of frequencies) and moves this peak up the frequency spectrum as the rocker is pushed down. Then as the rocker is pulled back, the wah moves the peak back down the spectrum, producing an 'ow' sound. A wah pedal can also be used as a type of tone control if the rocker is left set at one position.

There are also 'auto wah' pedals, which move the peak up or down in relation to the volume of the guitar signal. The natural volume swell of the note played causes the peak to move up the spectrum and as the note dies, the peak moves back down again.

Controls

In this case, very basic: a rocker pedal and a bypass switch to turn the effect on and off.

Placement

Wahs are usually placed very early in the signal chain. However, the effect can also be used after an overdrive or distortion pedal to create a thicker sound.

right *The Cry Baby Wah is the modern version made by Dunlop of the classic Vox Cry Baby.*
far right *The Electro-Harmonix Smallstone Phaser is another modern version of a classic effect.*

PHASERS

Type: Modulation

Phasers have a characteristic sweeping, 'whooshing' sound. The effect can be quite subtle on a clean guitar sound. It is created by automatically moving notches (the opposite of a peak: that is, cuts in level across a narrow range of frequencies) up and down the frequency spectrum, at a set rate. Phasers space the notches evenly across the frequency spectrum — an important difference from flanging, a delay-based effect (see below) where the notches are harmonically related.

Controls

Speed or rate: modifies how fast the notches are moved; speeds up or slows down the sweeping sound.
Depth: modifies how far across the frequency spectrum the notches are moved.
Resonance: modifies the level of the frequency peaks. This adds a more colourful overtone to the sound.

Placement

Gives a more subtle effect on a clean sound and a more obvious 'jet plane' sound when placed after a distortion or overdrive. Is often placed before a compressor, as this evens out the volume variation that can be created by the phasing effect.

COMPRESSION

Type: Level/dynamics control

A compressor is commonly used in recording to control the sound level, making loud passages quieter and quiet passages louder. This is useful in that it allows the sound to be heard clearly in the mix, but it is rarely an 'obvious' effect to the untrained ear. Compression is generally applied to a guitar to give clean sustain. The louder part of a note is cut in volume, then as the note fades away, the volume is gradually boosted.

Controls

Threshold/sensitivity: sets the level above which the volume is cut, and below which volume is boosted.

Attack: controls how fast the unit responds to volume increases.

Decay: controls how slowly the unit responds to decreasing volume.

Tone: compensates for a perceived treble loss, actually caused by the smoother volume dynamics.

Volume (or level): allows you to set a level to match the general loudness when the effect is bypassed.

Placement

Usually compression should be first in the signal chain, but sometimes you might want to place it after filter effects such as wah pedals or phasers, which can reduce volume at some settings. Placing a compressor after these effects helps even out volume differences.

OVERDRIVE, DISTORTION & FUZZ

Type: Distortion

The intention of these effects is to produce the sound of an overdriven valve amplifier, pushed well into clipping where the sound starts to distort. This is the most commonly used guitar effect of all.

Overdrive is usually obtained with a technique called soft clipping, where gain is reduced beyond the clip-

ping point, giving a smoother, more natural-sounding effect with even-order harmonics (those harmonically related to the note).

Distortion uses hard clipping, producing a harsher sound with odd-order harmonics. There is usually more gain here than with overdrive.

Fuzz is the original distortion effect, characterized by extreme levels of drive and odd-order harmonics.

top *The Boss CS-3 is a popular foot pedal compressor.*

above *The Ibanez TS9 Tube Screamer is one of the smoothest-sounding overdrive pedals ever made.*

above *The Boss*
DS-1 Distortion pedal can itself be
driven hard for a harsher distortion sound.

Controls

Gain/drive: controls the amount of overdrive.

Tone: compensates for additional highs created by the clipping process. There are sometimes expanded tone controls, such as bass, middle and treble.

Volume/level: balances the effect volume with the bypassed level. Also used to boost the signal for solos.

Placement

Overdrive is usually placed after a compressor in the signal chain, to produce a more sustained overdrive sound, but it will generally be placed before time-based effects like delays and reverb.

GRAPHIC EQUALIZERS

Type: EQ/tone

This effect is designed to give more tone control than is possible with the guitar or amplifier controls. A graphic equalizer uses sliders to control the level of specific fixed frequencies, called bands. They provide a graphic representation of the overall frequency response.

Controls

Frequency sliders: one per frequency to be modified.

Level control: allows you to compensate for any overall loudness changes made by the tone changes.

Placement

Equalizers can be placed almost anywhere in the signal chain, but are usually placed after compressors.

OCTAVE DIVIDERS

Type: Pitch-based

Octave dividers are simple pitch-shifters which copy the signal and then change the pitch of the copy so that it's one or two octaves below the signal at the input. The pitch-shifted copy is combined with the original signal. Octave dividers only work on one note at a time, becoming confused if they encounter more. The octaved signal is a square wave, which is similar to a distorted sound.

Controls

Range: sets how many octaves below the original the generated signal is.

Octave level: sets the level of the generated signal.

Level: sets the level of the combined signal.

Placement

Octave dividers work best after compressors as they are more stable with a steady level.

below *The Boss OC-3 Super Octave modern divider*
pedal is one that can be used to work
on more than a single note
at a time.

PITCH-SHIFTERS

Type: Pitch-based

This effect adds one or more pitch-shifted voices to the notes you're playing, similar to an octave divider or harmonizer. With pitch shifters, however, you set the harmony voices to fixed intervals, such as: up seven semitones, or down five semitones.

The pitch shifter has its uses, for example, shifting a pitch an octave higher; this works well for a modern-sounding 12-string emulation.

Controls

Shift amount: for each voice, sets the interval to shift the pitch.

Fine-tune: is set for each voice; allows you to de-tune a voice slightly to give a thicker sounding mix.

Voice level: is set for each voice; allows you to mix the harmonies with the original signal, assigning each its own level in the mix.

Level: controls the overall level.

Placement

As with harmonizers, will work best placed after compression and overdrive pedals but before time-based effects like delays and reverb.

HARMONIZERS

Type: Pitch-based

Harmonizers add one or more voices (pitch-shifted copies of what you are playing) to the notes you're already playing, similar to an octave divider or pitch shifter, the difference being that a harmonizer offers 'intelligent' chord-based harmonies. This allows you to play a line in a specific key and have one or more guitars playing harmony with you — in key.

Harmonizers use digital techniques that preserve the tone and timbre of your playing. This means the guitars in harmony sound a lot like the original guitar. They may even allow you to set your own chord intervals and apply random pitch variations or corrections to add extra realism to harmonies.

The notes generated are determined by the key (you set this) and the note you play. You could, for example, set harmonies to be a 3rd and a 5th, in the key of C major; the harmony intervals will change to make sure the harmony lines are always in the C major scale.

Controls

Key: sets what key the harmony is in

Interval: is set for each voice added; determines the interval the voice plays in relation to the original note.

Fine-tune: is set for each voice; allows you to de-tune a voice slightly to give a thicker sounding mix.

Voice level: set for each voice; allows you to mix the harmonies with the original signal, assigning each its own level in the mix.

Level: controls the overall level.

below *The Eventide Ultra-Harmonizer is rack-mounted, with multiple format corrected voices and a variety of other effects.*

Placement

Works best placed after compression and overdrive pedals, but before time-based effects like delays and reverb.

PITCH BEND

Type: Pitch-based

This is a digital effect designed to emulate a whammy bar via a rocker pedal. This is done by using a pitch shifter whose degree of shift is controlled by the rocker pedal. The output will feature only the sound effect. These effects are often combined with other digital pitch-based effects, such as vibrato or basic harmonizer options.

Controls

Bend range: this sets how far the pitch is bent.

Placement

The pitch bend is placed after compression, but before overdrive and time-based effects such as delays and reverb. Placing it after overdrive is also a viable option, however.

VIBRATO

Type: Modulation

Vibrato smoothly varies the pitch between slightly flat and sharp. This is similar to the fingerboard technique of string bending, moving a tremolo, or the effect gained using a rotary speaker. Vibrato is obtained by modulating the pitch of a signal. Some Fender amps have an effect labelled 'vibrato' but this is actually volume modulation, or tremolo.

Controls

Rate and depth: affects how fast and how far the pitch is changed.
Delay: often the effect is triggered automatically, and this sets how long the delay takes to reach the set depth.

Placement

Modulation effects work best placed after compression and overdrive pedals but before time-based effects like delays and reverb.

FLANGER

Type: Modulation

Flangers mix a varying delayed signal with the original sound to produce a series of notches in the frequency response – an effect similar to a phaser but with more resonance. The important difference between flanging and phasing is that a flanger produces a large number of notches, and the peaks between those notches are harmonically (musically) related. A phaser produces a small number of notches that are evenly spread across the frequency spectrum, and when there is high resonance, you get a 'jet plane' effect.

Controls

Speed or rate: controls how fast notches are moved.
Depth: controls how far through the frequency spectrum the notches are moved.
Resonance: controls the level of the frequency peaks.

Placement

A flanger is usually placed after compression and overdrive, but before time-based effects like delays and reverb.

below *The Boss BF-3 Flanger pedal features tap tempo, gated flanging and stereo outputs.*

CHORUS
Type: Modulation
The chorus effect works the same way as flanging and has a similar sound. However, it uses a longer delay than flanging, so there is a perception of 'spaciousness', which is particularly good for stereo. There is also little or no feedback, so the effect is more subtle. Vibrato mixes a varying delayed signal with the original to produce a large number of harmonically-related notches in the frequency response.

Controls
Speed or rate: controls how fast the notches are moved.

Depth: controls how far through the frequency spectrum the notches are moved.

Pre-delay: modifies the delay time.

Tone controls: sometimes available.

Intensity/effect/mix: monitors the level of the delayed signal, and consequently the depth of the frequency notches.

Placement
Chorus is placed usually after compression and overdrive, but before time-based effects such as delays and reverb.

NOISE GATE
Type: Level/dynamics
A noise gate, in its simplest form, is merely a switch that gets rid of the noise you hear during the quieter parts of a signal by muting (switching off) the sound. This effectively reduces the perceived level of noise in the signal. Although noise is usually masked (hidden) by the signal because, in comparison, it's normally at a much lower level, it can become noticeable and even quite annoying when the signal fades away in quieter sections of the music. A gate works by fading out the signal when it falls below a specific level (the threshold), muting both the signal and the noise. The fade prevents notes that fall below the threshold from being cut dead, giving the sound a natural decay.

There is often a separate trigger input and output. When a signal is applied to the trigger input, the gate opens (allows the signal through). This is particularly useful for guitar signals as you can use the pure, direct, guitar sound to control the gating of your noisy effects.

Controls
Threshold: sets the level below which volume is faded out.

Attack: controls how fast the gate starts working. Usually for guitar use you want it as fast as possible, and many guitar-specific units will not feature this control at all.

Decay: sets how fast the gate fades the volume.

Attenuation: sets how much the gate reduces the level.

left *The Boss CE-20 is one of Boss's dual pedals that have more options and abilities than the single pedals.*

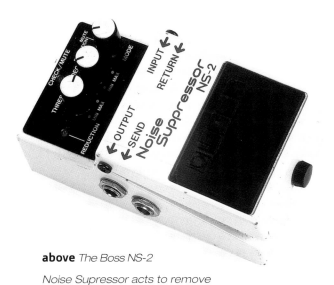

above *The Boss NS-2*
Noise Supressor acts to remove
hiss, hum and even feedback from a guitar sound.

Placement

A noise gate is always placed after most effects that produce noise, but before time-based effects (delays, reverb). If there is a trigger input, a compressor will sometimes go before it; the trigger output goes to the input of the next effect in the line.

LIMITER

Type: Level/dynamics control

This effect is similar to a compressor reducing high volumes, but a limiter does not boost low-level signals. A limiter is used to tame peaks in a sound without otherwise affecting the dynamics. It's not often used in guitar setups.

Controls

Threshold/sensitivity: sets the level above which volume is cut.

Attack: controls how fast the unit responds to volume increases.

Release: sets the level at which the effect turns off; is usually set a little lower than the threshold.

Volume (or level): allows you to set a level to match the general loudness when the effect is bypassed.

Placement

Anywhere in the signal chain where it is needed to control peaks.

VOLUME PEDAL

Type: Level/dynamics control

This is a simple device that allows you to control the volume level of the guitar signal with your foot. Some models permit the setting of a volume range, so you can adjust it downward to be at backing rhythm level and adjust upward to be at solo level.

Placement

The volume pedal is usually placed after a compressor. If it goes before the overdrive pedal, it will affect how much drive you get from the pedal; if placed after the overdrive, it will control only the level. It should always be placed before time-based effects, so the delay will sound natural.

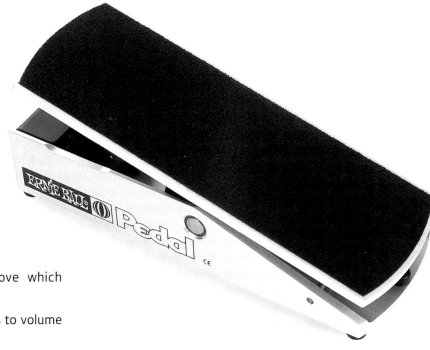

above *The impressively constructed Ernie Ball volume pedal is designed to take a lot of punishment.*

TREMOLO
Type: Modulation

A tremolo pedal modulates the guitar volume, similar to rapidly turning the volume control up and down. Different versions use different waveforms to modulate volume levels: sine waves produce a smooth effect with the volume fading in and fading out again; saw waveforms offer a less pulsating sound; and square waves turn the sound off and on very quickly. Some tremolo pedals allow you to select the waveform you want to use.

Controls

Speed: controls how fast the volume varies.
Depth: controls how much the volume varies.
Waveform: chooses the waveform you want to use for a specific modulation effect.

Placement

Tremolos work best placed after compression, but before time-based effects such as delays and reverb.

PANNING
Type: Modulation

Panning is a stereo effect that moves the signal from left to right. Basically, it is two tremolo effects, one for each of the left and right channels. These are linked so that when volume is high in one channel, it's low in the other, and vice versa.

Controls

Speed: controls how fast the sound moves from one side to the other.
Depth: controls how far the sound moves from one side to the other.
Waveform: selects the waveform for a specific modulation effect.

right *The DD-6, Boss's latest excellent digital delay, can create a delay of up to two seconds.*

Placement

The panning works best placed after compression, but before time-based effects such as delays and reverb.

DELAYS
Type: Time-based

Delay is an echo effect that repeats the original sound one or more times, contributing additional notes slightly later than the original; the effect is of a second guitarist playing along with the first. In earlier times, delays were tape-based, using a record head together with multiple playback heads. Modern delays sample the sound (record digitally) and store it in computer memory, so a perfect copy of the original sound can be played back repeatedly. Tape delays are less accurate, but due to the nature of magnetic tape, tend to lose some treble frequency. These are still prized by some for their 'warm' sound. More sophisticated units offer multiple taps (extra, shorter delays that appear before the main delay), with the option to position these taps anywhere between the left and right output channels for interesting stereo effects.

One popular stereo effect is 'ping pong delay', where the repeat effect sounds as if it's bouncing from left to right as it fades out. Another is 'doubling', where a single repeat with a short delay time (about 50 milliseconds) played at nearly the same level as the original note, sounds like two musicians playing the same thing in near-perfect unison.

Using effect pedals allows a guitarist to mix and match different brands and models of effect – and play around with the order.

By increasing the delay a little more (about 100 milliseconds), you get a slap-back echo effect. A very short delay time (1–12 milliseconds) produces phase cancellation at fixed frequencies (that is, the repeat note is heard so soon after the original that only a single sound registers). It effectively changes the tone.

Controls

Delay time: sets the length of time between the original sound and the repeat.
Delay level: sets the volume of the repeated sound.
Feedback/regeneration: sets the number of repeats.

Placement

Delay works best placed after all other effects, except reverb. Since digital units produce very little noise, they should always be placed after a noise gate. An effects 'tail' will persist after the gate has closed, which will create a more natural sound.

REVERB

Type: Time-based

Reverb (or reverberation) is the persistence of sound you hear in a room when it bounces around the walls for a while after the initial sound has stopped. It's made up of a very large number of repeats, which vary in level and tone as they progress.

Guitar amps with built-in reverb use a spring reverb, where one or more long springs are each connected to two transducers.

The first transducer acts as a speaker, playing the sound which then reverberates backward and forward through the spring. The second transducer picks up the resulting sound and mixes it back with the original signal.

Digital reverbs usually have various options for different-sized rooms and halls; studio effects such as plate, chamber and reverse reverbs; and sometimes emulations of guitar spring reverbs.

The better delay units may simulate the stage situation, featuring an early reflection of sound originating from the wall behind the player, which is heard first as a distinct, short echo.

Controls

Delay time: sets how long the reverb takes to die away to nothing.

Pre-delay: sets the length of time between the original sound and the first reflection.

Level: controls the overall volume and tone of the reverb.

Tone: changes the tonal balance of the reflections.

Early reflection delay: the length of time before the early reflection is heard.

Early reflection level: refers to the volume of the early reflection.

Placement

Reverb is usually the last effect in the signal chain. Since digital units produce very little noise, they should always be placed after a noise gate. An effects 'tail' usually persists after the gate has closed, which will create a more natural sound.

DI BOXES

Type: Other

In some circumstances a guitarist may want to take an electric guitar's output directly to a mixing console for recording or a PA system function, without the processing of an amplifier. Sometimes this is done at the same time as a mic'ed signal and both are mixed together for a range of tones. However, guitars plugged directly

into a mixing console do not sound very good, primarily due to the technical consideration of an impedance mismatch. DI (Direct Injection) boxes allow a guitarist to correct these problems and interface directly with the console. A DI-ed electric guitar will have a very clean tone with extra 'high end' (treble) not found with a mic'ed amplifier. It will often need some equalization to sound its best. While it is possible to process the DI-ed guitar sound with other effects, any overdrive and distortion effects will sound very harsh without the smoothing benefits of the amplifier.

Controls

DI boxes do not usually have any controls, but do sometimes have ground-lift switches, which help to eliminate ground loop problems.

ENHANCERS

Type: EQ/tone

Enhancers are used to make a signal stand out in a mix without raising the volume. They do this by taking the harmonics of the input signal, distorting them, then mixing them back at low levels with the original signal.

Some enhancers use sophisticated phase correction systems to achieve the same effect.

Controls

Low enhance: sets how much the low-frequency component of the signal is enhanced.

High enhance: sets the enhancement of the high-frequency component of the signal.

Level: sets an overall level for level balancing.

Placement

An enhancer will usually be last in the signal chain, although it may be placed before any time-based effects like delay and reverb.

left *A DI box is used to send a clean guitar sound directly to a mixing desk or recorder, without using an amp.*

left *The top quality Lexicon multi-effect units have most types of effect built into one box.*

MULTI-EFFECTS

It is increasingly common to find multi-effect units; these contain any number of effects in one convenient unit. This can be in the form of a floor unit with foot switches and rocker controls, or as a number of rack-mounted units with MIDI control, and any MIDI-capable foot switch.

The main attraction of multi-effect units is that effect configurations and settings can be stored in convenient memory locations called patches. When a patch is selected, it recalls all the different effects stored in the patch, their order of placement and all the individual settings used by each effect. These patches can then easily be changed via MIDI.

This capability can save a lot of the 'tap dancing' and knob tweaking necessary to control a number of separate floor pedals.

Many multi-effect units also contain modelled amplifiers and speaker simulators, often making this the only device needed for a gig; your multi-effect and guitar are plugged straight into the PA and monitor system. If you prefer to use only the effects, with your guitar amplifier and speakers onstage, you simply write your patches with amp and speaker simulations turned off.

Another advantage of multi-effect units is their cost-effectiveness — the price is many times less than buying all the loose effects individually. It is more of an initial outlay, however, and you cannot budget for one effect at a time as you can with single pedals.

One disadvantage of multi-effect units is that, for the beginner, it presents a steep learning curve when you purchase a variety of effects all at the same time. To get around this, you need to experiment with one effect at a time, learning how to use it competently before moving on to the next one. It is also possible that you will prefer a particular effect from a different manufacturer.

Most good multi-effect units will allow the guitarist to insert a separate pedal into an effect loop, then switch the loop — and thus the effect — in and out as required.

MODELLING EFFECTS

The advent of modelling technology has enabled manufacturers to make modelling effect units, where the sound and character of many vintage and popular effects are digitally emulated in one unit. While many purists still prefer the originals themselves, the majority of people who don't have access to the original effects will find they are a viable alternative for obtaining a specific sound.

In most cases the modelled effect will also have the benefits of modern-style patch settings and MIDI control. They are an advantage, too, in situations where you would prefer not to take your valuable vintage effect units to a gig.

CHAPTER 6

Guitar Setup &
MAINTENANCE

A well set-up and well-maintained guitar is a pleasure to play. It looks good, sounds good and stays in tune. You are able to learn faster and play better. Most importantly, it allows you to forget about the instrument itself and simply play music. This section tackles issues ranging from basic tasks such as cleaning and stringing to those which are often approached with fear, such as adjusting your truss rod.

CLEANING YOUR GUITAR

Cleaning and polishing a guitar are the first things every player should learn. This is the most basic maintenance task which, if done properly, will help retain or restore an instrument's looks and value.

If cleaning is carried out regularly from the time a new guitar is purchased, it remains a simple task, taking only a few minutes to keep things in top condition. Left too long, the minute deposits of sweat, grease, smoke and dust build up and harden, making the task a lot more difficult.

Cleaning tools

CLOTHS

Clean, soft, cotton cloths are best for cleaning an electric guitar. Polishes and cleaners can speed up the job, but the cloth is the only essential item. It could be a cloth bought specially for the job or an old T-shirt, as long as it's pure cotton and soft. Ideally, it should also be lint-free so it doesn't leave cotton particles behind as you're cleaning — if you've ever used a cheap yellow duster, you'll have encountered lint!

CLEANERS

The best all-round cleaner is naphtha (lighter fluid). Naphtha is strong enough to remove most build-up and grease on a guitar, and is gentle enough to use on virtually any finish without causing any damage.

You can use it to remove grease from an unfinished rosewood fingerboard, clean stubborn marks from a delicate vintage lacquer finish and to soak and clean metal hardware such as bridges and saddles.

POLISHES

Specialized guitar polishes are usually a combination of a very mild abrasive for lifting dirt and smoothing tiny scratches, a wax for shine and protection, and a liquid used to suspend the other ingredients and for the cleaning process.

Two things to avoid in your guitar polishes are silicone and oils. Both tend to make a finished guitar feel greasy, and they can enter cracks in the finish, penetrating the wood of the instrument, saturating it

Clean your guitar with some polish or cleaner and a soft cloth, bunched up into what is known as a 'tampon'.

and possibly making the finish lift. Silicone also tends to make any future guitar repair work, for example, refinishing or glueing, extremely difficult.

CLEANING

Make sure that dust and grit is blown or dusted off the guitar before you do anything, otherwise you will scratch the guitar by moving particles around over the finish as you clean or polish.

With a new or relatively clean instrument, it is a quick and easy job to wipe down the finish with your cloth to remove fingerprints or other marks. A little 'breath mist' will help remove the more stubborn marks. Take note also of the following tips:

* If the grime is a little more hardy or you want to polish out the tiny scratches that dull a finish, start with the guitar polish, following the manufacturer's instructions, since some polishes are applied and left to dry before removing, while others are removed immediately. Finish up with a clean cloth for best results.

* The purpose of polish is to remove only small amounts of grime while polishing – otherwise you will end up trapping the dirt below a layer of protective wax. Use some naphtha first to remove the grime, then follow up with either a clean cloth or with polish and then use the cloth.

Use a blade to scrape years of sweat and grime from the fingerboard. This will also smooth the fingerboard, removing small dents caused by wear.

* To clean an unfinished rosewood or ebony fingerboard, wipe it down with naphtha. If there is a lot of build-up on the surface, the edge of a utility knife blade will scrape off the worst. Three or so times a year, rub in a few drops of lemon oil with a small piece of cloth. Leave for a few minutes, then wipe off excess oil with a dry section of the cloth. Use the cloth only for this task.

STRINGING

Approximately 80–90% of a guitar's tone comes from the strings. They provide the fundamental sound; the guitar, pick-ups and amplifier merely 'colour' it. The strings are the single biggest cause of tuning, intonation, tone and playability problems, so caring for and changing them regularly will ensure top performance from your instrument. It will also help prevent many common guitar problems.

HOW OFTEN SHOULD YOU CHANGE STRINGS?

The durability of your strings depends on a myriad variables: the metals they are made of, how they're played, atmospherics, temperatures and how the strings are maintained. Personal preference plays a large part, as some players prefer the crisp, bright sound of brand-new strings, while others prefer the mellower sound of strings that have been 'played in'.

Believe it or not, the most important variable is your body chemistry and how this reacts with the metals of your strings. I have known people who have such corrosive body chemistry that strings that would usually last me a month will start corroding on their guitar within 24 hours!

As a general guideline, someone who plays once a day should be changing at least once a month. However, this does not mean that if you only play once a month you can play the same set of strings for 30 months! Unfortunately, once strings are tuned up and, more importantly, have been played once (even if just to tune them!), they start to age. Even for the most casual player, three months is stretching it.

MAKING STRINGS LAST

Most importantly, clean your strings after each playing session! Use a soft cloth to clean off excess moisture and consider using either a string-cleaning product or surgical spirits/isopropyl alcohol to wipe them down.

There are now some types of string that are coated with a thin polymer layer. This layer protects the string

Wiping down the top surface of the strings will make sure they last longer.

Wipe the underside of the strings and the fingerboard by sliding a soft cloth between the two.

The best way to clean strings is to wrap the cloth around each one and wipe it from top to bottom.

from any corrosive substances in the player's body chemistry, or in the air, while being so thin that it doesn't affect the tone in any significant way. While these strings are comparatively expensive, they generally last three to four times longer. Other durable strings are those that are gold-plated. These two types of string are also suitable for players who are allergic to the metals in the strings.

RESTRINGING YOUR GUITAR

The way in which your guitar is strung is important, and correct technique is often overlooked in favour of quicker methods. The reality is that correctly fitted strings will minimize the chances of your guitar going out of tune.

The simple secret of effective stringing is to get as short a length of string as possible. The less string you have wound around the tuning machine, the less string there is to stretch and settle.

1. Firstly, thread the strings through the bridge. Various bridges load strings differently: some load the strings through the guitar body, others through the back of the bridge behind the saddles, yet others have a

top *Strings are threaded through the back of a Stratocaster.*
above *Pull the strings through from the front of the guitar to make sure they seat properly before pulling them up to the headstock.*

tailpiece that's separated from the bridge. It does not really matter as it is usually easy to figure out where the strings go.

2. Start with the sixth string; pull the string up toward the headstock of the guitar and thread it

through the top of the hole in the tuning machine. Leave enough slack to wind two turns of string around the post, no more. Do not wrap the string around the post by hand from the top. While this is quicker than winding it on by turning the tuning machine key, it often results in a twisted string.

top *Stringing a three-a-side headstock, beginning from the outside strings and moving inward.*
above *Stringing a six-a-side headstock beginning with the 6th string and finishing with the 1st string.*

hole; the second winding should wrap beneath it. This ensures that the string end is gripped firmly by the two windings when under tension. While winding, ensure that the string falls into the correct nut slot and seats itself correctly in the saddle.

4. If you've judged the length of the string correctly, the string should be near tension, needing no more than $1/2$–1 turn more to bring the string to pitch.

Repeat the process for all other strings. You'll find that it's easier to fit the strings in order, so that those already fitted don't get in the way of subsequent strings. This means that if your guitar has a Strat-style headstock with all six tuning machines on one side, you will fit the strings in the order: 6 – 5 – 4 – 3 – 2 – 1. If your guitar has a Les Paul-style headstock with three tuning machines on each side, the order will be: 6 – 1 – 5 – 2 – 4 – 3.

Tune all the strings to pitch and then stretch them a little by pulling them up, away from the body of the guitar — not too much, only 3 or 4cm ($1\frac{1}{2}$in). This both

This puts added stress on the string while under tension and may shorten its life span.

3. Turn the tuning machine to wind the string on the post. Ensure that the first winding wraps around the post above the string protruding through the

stretches the string a little, and pulls the windings tight on the tuning machine posts (both of which would happen over a day or so anyway; this simply speeds things up a little). Once you have done this with all six strings, tune the guitar again and repeat until the tuning holds. You should find the tuning to be

fairly stable, and bar one or two tweaks over the next few hours, you will have avoided the usual tune-up, play for 30 seconds, tune-up, play routine.

Stretching the strings by pulling them up away from the fingerboard ensures that the tuning settles quickly.

LOCKING TUNING MACHINES

These wonderful devices take the less-windings-is-better idea to the extreme by clamping the string in place at the tuning machine. This ensures that the only string-winding around the post is the half-turn or so used to tune up to pitch.

FLOATING TREMOLO BRIDGES

These bridges do not require a ball on the end of the string on the bridge side; instead they clamp the bare string into place.

Instead of cutting the ball end off, you could install the string backward, with the ball end on the tuning machine side. Then simply cut the string to the correct length from the tuning machine side, clamp into place and tune normally.

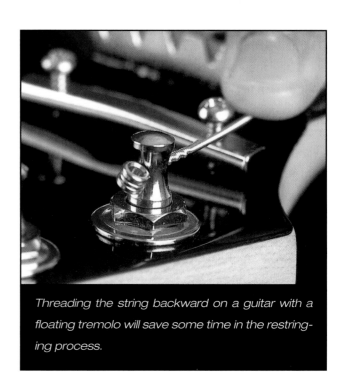

Threading the string backward on a guitar with a floating tremolo will save some time in the restringing process.

TRUSS RODS

Many guitarists view truss rods with fear. And rightly so — warped necks and stripped or broken truss rods are a few of the results of a heavy hand. One simple rule: if you're not comfortable doing these adjustments yourself, DON'T. Refer it rather to your trusted luthier. If you haven't been scared off at this point, then with care and patience and the instructions below, you can succeed in doing it yourself.

Truss rod adjustment

First, let me dispel one myth I've seen do damage to dozens of necks in the last few years: the truss rod is not for adjusting your action! While it does affect the action of an instrument, this is a byproduct rather than the reason for adjusting. The truss rod is for adjusting the curve of the neck to avoid fret buzzes.

It might seem that a neck should be flat from first to last fret, but due to the way strings vibrate in an elliptical pattern, there needs to be a slight relief (gap) downward (away from the strings) between the 12th and 1st frets. If the neck curves up in the middle without enough relief, this is called a bow.

CHECKING RELIEF OF GUITAR NECK

Tune your guitar to the exact tuning you use. If the tension is incorrect, you will get a faulty impression of the curvature of the neck. Hold your guitar in the playing position. Push the low E-string down on the first fret and the highest fret simultaneously and inspect the relief between the bottom of the string and the top of the seventh and eighth frets. There should be a $\frac{1}{2}$mm gap (not all guitars are equal so some will need a little more or less than this). Also, if you play harder, you may need more relief than someone with a light touch.

By pushing the string down on the first and last frets, you are able to inspect the neck relief; there should be a tiny gap between string and fret.

Adjusting a truss rod using an Allen key: turning clockwise tightens the rod while anticlockwise loosens it.

ADJUSTING TRUSS ROD

Find the truss-rod nut. This will be located at one end of the neck or the other (usually behind the nut or at the base of the neck). Remove the truss-rod cover if there is one.

Use the correct tool to do any required adjustment as incorrect tools may ruin your truss-rod nut. Your tool will be a spanner, Allen key (hex wrench) or, in some cases, a screwdriver. If you don't have the correct tool, get one or stop right there.

Note that many American-made guitars will have imperial-size nuts, which in many cases are similar in size to their metric counterparts, but although these may be almost right, they will cause damage if used.

✳ If the relief is insufficient (less than 0.5mm clearance at the 7th and 8th frets, or none at all), loosen the truss rod a quarter-turn in an anticlockwise direction.

✳ If the relief is too large, gently give the truss-rod nut a one-quarter turn in a clockwise direction. Repeat if necessary.

✳ Do not make any adjustments more than a quarter turn at a time.

✳ Check the relief at the 7th and 8th frets again, and if it is still not right, repeat the process.

Something is WRONG and you need to take your guitar to a professional luthier if the truss-rod nut:

✳ requires large amounts of adjustment

✳ makes loud grating or creaking sounds

✳ turns with no resistance

✳ turns with too much resistance.

Special Notes

Double truss rods These beasts are very tricky but quite rare! Don't even think about it, unless you have a degree in engineering and lots of practice on cheap, disposable guitars with double truss rods.

Old or 'reissue' Fender guitars These often have the truss-rod nut at the base of the neck, obscured by the scratchplate. Here, you need to remove the strings, remove the neck, adjust the truss-rod nut, put the neck back, replace the strings, re-tune, and check the relief. Then the process begins over again.

Left-hand thread truss rods These are rare, but need more attention and care to get right.

If you are able to make the adjustments yourself, put the truss-rod cover back and play. Check it again in 24 hours. The truss may have 'settled' a bit and will need an eighth of a turn or so to tweak it to perfection again.

ACTION

Action — the height of the strings above the frets — is the most important setting affecting playability. A guitar that has a large space between the strings and the fingerboard is said to have a 'high action'; if the strings are close to the frets, the guitar has a 'low action'.

The exact setting of a guitar's action is mostly an individual player's choice. A guitar with a higher action is louder, has better tone but is harder to play. With low action, the same guitar is easier to play, but has less tone and volume, and is more prone to fret buzzes.

How high should the strings be?

Using feeler gauges (thin metal strips used for gauging the size of a gap, obtainable from any hardware store), measure the distance between the bottom of the string and the body fret (where the neck joins the body — about the 15th fret for most electric guitars). As a good rough indication of what the action should be:

Bass E string = 2.4mm

Treble E string = 1.6mm

You can add or subtract about 0.5mm to these measurements for a high or low action respectively.

Adjusting bridge action

Electric guitars have some kind of screw, Allen key or thumbwheel on the bridge enabling you to set the bridge action.

❊ Strats and most other guitars have individual screws/Allen bolts for each saddle

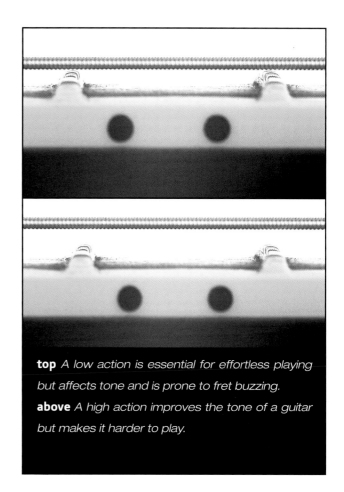

top *A low action is essential for effortless playing but affects tone and is prone to fret buzzing.*
above *A high action improves the tone of a guitar but makes it harder to play.*

above *An Allen key is being used here to adjust the height of a saddle on a Stratocaster, which in turn sets the action of the string.*

* Les Pauls and many arch-top electrics have two thumbwheels, one on either side of the bridge
* some older and vintage re-issue Telecasters have one saddle for every two strings
* most locking tremolo systems have two large screws or bolts for the entire bridge.

Once located, turn these and you will see the bridge or saddle move up or down (depending on the direction you turn them).

Nut action

First of all, make sure the bridge action is set correctly before tackling the nut action. Then make sure that your nut action actually needs adjustment by playing a few notes at the top of the neck. If the nut is too low, you will hear string buzz on the open-string notes (unfretted), but not on the fretted notes. If it is too high, the action will be stiffer than you'd like near the nut, but will be easier to play slightly higher up the neck. Bear in mind that there is no universally correct nut action, but your preferences as a player affect how low or how high it should be.

top *Setting action on a Tune-O-Matic Gibson Les Paul bridge.*

above *Adjusting the bridge action of a floating bridge with an Allen key.*

MEASURING NUT ACTION

Ideally, the nut action for each string should be set so that the gap between the string and the first fret on open notes is a fraction smaller than the gap between the string and the second fret when you push down at the first fret. So you need to compare these two gaps using your feeler gauges.

To do this, fret the string at the first fret. Then slide different feeler gauges into the gap between the second fret and the string until you get one (or a combination) that fits snugly without being too tight. If the gauge pushes up the string, use a thinner gauge.

Now use that same gauge to check the gap between the string and the first fret. It should be slightly tighter. If the fit is a lot tighter, the nut action

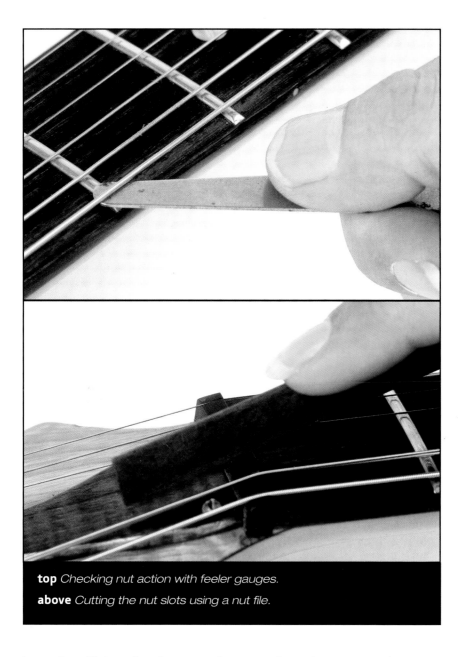

top *Checking nut action with feeler gauges.*
above *Cutting the nut slots using a nut file.*

Loosen the first string (only the first – you need to keep as much of the normal tension on the neck as possible), so that you can lift the string out of the slot and move it aside to rest on the top of the nut, or in the second string's slot (on top of the second string). Then start filing the slot deeper, using a nut file or a triangular needle file. File at a downward angle from the fingerboard side of the nut toward the headstock to keep the slot at a slight angle. This will ensure that the string moves easily through the slot when tuning and avoids the possibility of nut intonation problems. Frequently stop filing and put the string in place, checking the height at the first fret with your gauges to avoid cutting too deep. Once you have attained the correct depth, replace the string and retune.

Repeat this process for the second and third strings. To do the fourth through sixth strings, use a small rounded file, otherwise repeat the same process.

is too low. If there is a large gap between the string and the gauge, then the nut action is too high.

LOWERING NUT

If you find that the nut action is too high, you need to cut the slots deeper. For cutting the slots you will need a set of calibrated nut files or a set of needle files. Nut files are ideal as they are specially made to easily cut a round-bottomed slot of the exact width needed for the string. However, they are fairly expensive specialized tools, and the same job can be done with a set of inexpensive needle files — provided care is taken.

RAISING STRING HEIGHT AT NUT

If you find that the string height at the nut is too low, or you have cut the string slots too deep, the height at the nut can be increased.

A shim (a thin spacer) of mahogany or maple veneer can be placed beneath the nut. To do this, remove the nut, cut a shim to the same width and glue it to the bottom of the nut, then glue the nut to the neck. Once the nut has been shimmed sufficiently, the string height can then be lowered, if necessary, using the same procedure as described above.

INTONATION

You could experience the problem where the notes go progressively out of tune as you move up the fingerboard. The open chords sound fine, but the same chords played as barré further down the neck are out. If your strings are in good condition, chances are you need to set your intonation.

Setting intonation

The pitch of a vibrating string is determined by its length, diameter, mass and tension. When you fret a note you are effectively reducing the length of the string (scale), thus raising its pitch. Unfortunately, when you push the string down to the fret, the string is stretched; this raises the tension and sharpens the

above *A tuner is used here to check the intonation at the 12th fret.*

note slightly. This effect increases as you fret closer to the bridge (shorter scale lengths are more sensitive to variations in tension). To compensate for this, you can increase the scale length by moving the saddle further away from the nut.

Tune the guitar to pitch and check the intonation of each string separately. First play the note on the 12th fret (one octave above the open string). Then play the 12th fret harmonic (the same note). A digital tuner is likely to be more accurate than your ear, so use it if you have one.

* If both notes have exactly the same pitch, the intonation is correct.
* If the pitch of the fretted note is the sharper of the two, the saddle should be moved away from the nut (increasing scale length).
* If the pitch of the fretted note is the flatter of the two, the saddle must be moved toward the nut (decreasing scale length).

Adjusting the saddle

Arch-top bridges These often have a loose bridge that can be moved freely backward and forward; generally they need to be angled slightly toward the nut on the treble side of the bridge.

Floating bridges Set the treble E string first. Push and hold the arm down, loosen the Allen bolt at the very front of the saddle, move the saddle in the desired direction and tighten the bolt. Release the arm and re-tune (that is, loosen the lock nut, re-tune all the strings, and tighten the locks again).

Check the intonation once more and repeat the sequence if necessary. Then move to the second saddle and repeat the entire process. This needs to be done for each saddle.

Gibson-style Tune-O-Matic bridges Each string sits on a small metal insert that acts as its own saddle. These can be moved backward and forward individually by means of small screws located at the back of the bridge.

With an arch-top bridge, intonation is adjusted by moving the bridge.

The saddle of a floating bridge is loosened to move it for setting the intonation.

Tune-O-Matic bridge saddles are moved by using a small slotted screwdriver.

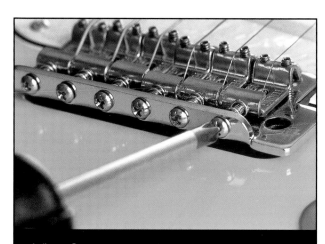

Adjust Stratocaster-style bridge saddles via the Philips screws at the back of the bridge.

You can start with any string, in any order. Just remember to re-tune between each and every adjustment.

Stratocaster-style bridges Small screws at the back of the base plate control the position of the individual saddles. It makes no difference which string you do first, but again, re-tune between each adjustment.

Vintage Telecaster-style bridges The saddles each carry a pair of strings, allowing adjustment in pairs. The intonation settings are always a compromise, though. Consider upgrading the bridge to one that has six separate saddles; then the setting method is the same as for a Strat-style bridge.

General Points to Note

* Re-tune between every single adjustment. By moving the saddle you change the pitch and tension of the entire string, which will affect the intonation readings.
* If you change the gauge (thickness) of the strings, or change to an altered tuning, your intonation will probably need adjustment.
* Sometimes, a different type or make of string will change the intonation (different compounds have different masses and tensions).

TRAVELLING WITH YOUR GUITAR

If you ever have to travel with your guitar by plane or car, or perhaps even ship it to a destination, you need to take a few specific precautions to ensure you have your guitar in one piece at the end of the journey.

GENERAL PRECAUTIONS

Buy a guitar case This should go without saying, but it never ceases to amaze me how many people will spend large amounts of money on their instrument, only to buy a cheap padded bag to protect it. Get as good a case as you can afford. Moulded cases are good for most situations, but if you plan to allow others to transport your instrument, a heavy-duty flight case is better.

Pack the case properly Make sure there is no movement, particularly at the headstock. Pack material in any spaces between the guitar and the sides of the case. Place wads of material under the headstock — enough to lift the neck 5mm (¼in) off the neck rest.

Do not loosen the strings String tension creates a balance along the length of the body vs. the stress

Eric Clapton's onetime flight case – an essential item
if others are transporting your guitar!

TRAVEL BY CAR

Never put your guitar in the boot of your car
Temperatures inside may exceed 65°C (149°F) which
can cause tremendous damage to your guitar.

Secure it If you keep the guitar on the back seat,
make sure it won't fly forward if you brake sharply.

Acclimatization When bringing the guitar in from a
cold car to a warm room (and vice versa), let it warm
up for an hour or so before opening the case. This will
prevent tiny cracks from developing in the finish.

SHIPPING

Find the best cardboard shipping box you can at a guitar store. Pack padding material around your case to
ensure it does not move around inside the box. Use
straps, or at the very least, some packing tape to close
the box. Remember to insure your guitar for the full
replacement value.

AIR TRAVEL

Carry your guitar on as hand luggage – even if it
means your bag with toothbrush and personals has to
go in the luggage hold! This is your single biggest pre-
caution – apart from damage to the instrument, there
is always the possibility of delays, loss or theft when
the guitar goes through normal baggage handling.

Some airlines can be reluctant to allow you to carry
on your guitar because of size or security concerns. An
electric guitar in a gig bag might not cause a problem,
but a large guitar in its case may well exceed the carry-
on size limit.

For carry-on purposes, moulded, shaped, lightweight cases work best. Of the selection of hard cases
available to you, they are the smallest and lightest. The
case hardware should be the cam-lock type, which is
difficult to unlatch accidentally. While a heavy-duty
flight case is preferable if you are forced to put the
guitar in the luggage hold, a well-fitting moulded case
will provide sufficient protection.

created by the weight of the tuning machines and
neck: your guitar is more at risk with the strings loose.

Fragile stickers If someone else is to handle your guitar at any point, do not assume they will know that it
needs special care.

Identification tags Put stickers on with your name,
address and telephone numbers.

CHAPTER 7

On
STAGE

Whether you want to be the next multi-platinum-selling artist or are content with the occasional gig playing with (or for) friends, eventually you will perform in front of others. There is much you need to know to be a performing musician — and the more you know, the better.

JOINING A BAND

Once a guitarist has bought a guitar and an amplifier, hopefully had some lessons and practised faithfully, and learned how to play some songs and emulated his or her heroes, the next stage virtually suggests itself: you need to find others to play with — and this is the best way to further your knowledge and improve your skills. If you're lucky, you may already have friends who have the same musical tastes, play instruments and want to start a band. If not, and you are striking out on your own, it's time to reach out.

While it's not always easy to find fellow musicians, there are avenues you can follow to do so. Find and reply to advertisements in your local paper, music shops, on-line communities, schools, colleges, universities as well as the back pages of music magazines. Make contacts by asking people you know, salesmen in your favourite music shop, your guitar teacher, and by visiting local jam or open mic nights.

Once you have learned to play your guitar with competence, joining a band is the next logical step!

Consider placing advertisements in these places yourself. List your instrument, style and influences, and the type of musicians or band you're looking for. If you haven't been playing all that long, mention it, as it lets potential band mates know what your level of playing is. If you have equipment and transport, mention this too. Most importantly, make sure you include all the contact details a person will need to get in touch with you and the hours they can do so.

left *The Rolling Stones, still going strong today, have been performing on stage since the early 1960s.*

If you are fortunate enough to end up with a choice of people to play with, spend some time with each person, individually, to find out if you get on with them all and also what direction they are hoping the band will take. Then make your decision based on who will fit best with your ideas.

REHEARSING

Once you have formed or joined a band, you will begin rehearsals, which can be held anywhere you can fit yourselves, your instruments, amplification and any other accessories and still leave room to play.

‎hearsal space

‎‎‎‎ ‎‎‎‎‎‎‎‎ ‎‎d be either in an isolated location or
‎‎‎‎‎‎‎‎‎‎‎ ‎‎ugh so that your rehearsals do

not become a problem for the neighbourhood. Many bands use a basement or garage, but local schools, community centres and even churches may hire out their halls for reasonable rates.

The problem with these options is the lack of PA equipment, which will either need to be hired for each practice or purchased outright. The other option is a dedicated rehearsal studio, where PA equipment is often supplied as part of the price. The studio may also hire out drum kits as well as guitar and bass amplification, saving you from having to transport and set up your own gear every time you rehearse.

Discipline

Impose some discipline on your band rehearsals. They should be on the same days and at the same time every week; this avoids confusion and establishes a routine. Practise each set of songs as one continuous performance and take breaks in-between sets, exactly as you would in a performance.

Personal practice

It is important to note that the band rehearsal time should be exactly that: band rehearsal. It is not the time for you to be learning how to play your part while the other members stand around waiting for you — particularly if you are paying for your rehearsal space. Spend time at home learning and practising your parts as well as furthering your playing. Also spend time alone, or with just the vocalist or keyboard player, to work on new material which you can then take to the rest of the band at rehearsal.

GIGGING

Perform live at every opportunity. Start with a few short shows for your friends or relatives. Offer to play at parties, functions, weddings and any other small event for free. Approach your school, college or community centre for performance opportunities.

If you expect your first few performances to be shaky, work under a different band name until everyone is experienced and comfortable with playing live. This will allow your band to make as many mistakes as are needed in order to polish your act to a 'professional' quality! Once you have some experience under your belt and feel confident, approach local venues and agents for bookings.

Set lists

Think of your set as something that can be worked on in the same way you work on your playing skills. You should pay attention to every detail of your show, as the audience will respond to a band who takes the trouble to do this.

Create predetermined sets that the whole band know inside out. They should be arranged like a song, with dynamics. For example: start with two or three of your faster, more vibrant songs, then slow down the pace for two songs, before picking up the pace again for a few songs, finally ending the set with a full energy anthem. A dynamic set is a lot easier to listen to than one that starts out at a certain tempo and continues that way until the end of the set.

Try to take into account instrument changes. If you play four songs with your Gibson Les Paul and two with a Stratocaster, arrange them so that you only have to change guitars once.

Work on what happens between songs — as the spaces are part of the set. Fill the spaces. While you could possibly finish the song, wait for the keyboard player to change patches, have a few arbitrary words from the vocalist, then start the next song in the set, a better option would be: drums and bass continuing with a variation of the song's theme fairly quietly, filling in the space behind the vocalist while the keyboard player gets ready, then the drummer bringing the whole band into the next song with a short fill.

Setting up

This can sometimes take almost as long as your first set, especially if you are supplying the PA, so get into a routine where you can cut down the time. Pack your vehicles in a sensible way: if you set up your PA speakers on stage first, make sure they are packed in last, so they can be the first things unloaded at the venue. Take care if you're offloading your gear into a crowded venue; punters don't take kindly to having flight cases bounced off them!

Familiarize yourselves with the order in which gear is set up. If it's easiest to set up the drum kit first and build everything round it, then do exactly that every time. Make sure that each member of the band knows what his/her specific tasks are; the entire band trying to set up the vocal mic can only delay matters. Give everyone a job and let them get on with it.

Be professional

START ON TIME

If your posters advertised you starting at 21:00, do so. Don't keep the 20 paying customers waiting while you hope for a sudden rush of people at 21:30.

SET LIST

If you're doing two 45-minute sets with a 30-minute break, let the owner/manager know and stick to it. Club owners prefer to know what to expect, especially if they have hired a disc jockey to provide entertainment during your band's breaks.

QUIET TUNING

Tuning aloud is not something that the audience needs, or wants to hear you do after every few songs. There are tuners available that allow you to tune with no volume.

BACKUP INSTRUMENTS

Occasionally you may break a string in the middle of a song. Have at least one backup guitar set up – it's a lot quicker to change guitars than it is to change strings.

AUDIENCE COMMUNICATION

Have one front person who does the speaking, usually the vocalist. Don't let the stage become a free-for-all with everyone talking, as the audience will find it difficult to focus on anyone. Everyone in the band should cue off the front person, and only talk when that person talks to them.

MAKE EYE CONTACT

Keep your head up and make eye contact while playing.

DON'T GIVE IT AWAY, PART I

No one in the audience knows the songs as well as you do, and they will not notice even the worst mistakes. So don't give it away with a grimace or by glaring at the guilty band member. Keep on playing – the worst thing you can do is grind to a halt.

DON'T GIVE IT AWAY, PART II

Don't play the first few chords of the next song before you actually start playing it. Guitarists often do this to check volume, tuning, or sound – but it doesn't sound good from the audience's perspective.

While being a gripping live performer, Courtney Love's outrageous on-stage and off-stage antics have affected her career negatively.

KEEP GOOD TIME

Get the band tight musically — that is, playing together well and in control of your timing. Rushing or dragging the beat makes a band sound amateurish and kills the 'feel'. Fix this by practising to a metronome.

BAND PROMOTION

Be organized, be different and be persistent. Realize that your band is a business and treat it as such — you will be rewarded by having a successful band. Your objective is to expose as many people as possible to your band and there are an almost infinite number of methods to do this.

Look around you at other businesses and see the methods they use to promote themselves. Most of the standard business promotions will work for a band.

Flyers

Probably the first thing every band does is distribute flyers; they are cheap and they work.

Business cards

While not quite as cheap to produce as flyers, these are just as effective and much more businesslike. The fact is, people generally keep business cards, while they rarely keep flyers.

Don't forget that there are two sides to a business card and it's not that expensive to print a slogan, demo offer, or any other pertinent information on the back of your cards.

Press releases

This is a simple statement about what you are doing at any given time. Send press releases to local newspapers, radio stations, and anyone else you want to keep informed about your band.

Suitable information would be: when you are involved with a big show, when you're recording a new demo, and so on. Start keeping copies of not only your originals, but of any clippings from newspapers that print your items.

Press packages

Eventually you will want to put together a press package for your band. The standard is to have a 20x25cm (8x10in) black-and-white photo of either yourself (if you are a solo artist) or the band together. Consider it an investment and hire a professional photographer. Along with a photo you'll need a brief biography of each member of the band as well as an overall biography on the band itself; a short introduction about who you are, where you come from and where you're going; what your experience is and what your purpose and goals are.

Networking

Make friends with your local reporters, disc jockeys, the receptionist who answers the phone at the radio station and newspaper, anyone who might be able to assist you.

Along with your press release, send a handwritten note or card thanking them in advance for passing along your information. If you have a demo, send them a copy with a handwritten note asking for their feedback. If you have T-shirts, send them one. Whatever you send them, always send along the handwritten note, either thanking them or asking for their opinion on a particular matter. Generally, because they are made to feel that their opinion matters, you stay in their mind and they will be inclined to do more for you.

Don't waste their time, however. Don't become a nuisance and send them things too often. You need to appreciate that these are very busy people, so it's better to only send information to them when you have something to report.

Demo CDs

Demo tapes and CDs are excellent marketing tools, providing they are good enough to show off your material. Once again this is an investment, and people are used to good sound quality demos, so it is well worth saving up the money to have your material recorded in a professional studio.

PA speakers come in all shapes and sizes, but all have one thing in common — they are made for higher volumes.

PA SYSTEMS

At some point you will encounter a public address (PA) system and often you will need to be the one controlling it or, at the very least, have to relate to the person who is. This amplification system takes a source signal (speech or music) at the input and makes it louder at the output. In its most basic form, it comprises three components. These are: a sound source, an amplifier and a loudspeaker.

The sound source produces an electrical signal that represents the sound, and can be a transducer such as a microphone, a line-level instrument like a keyboard, or a playback device such as a CD player. The amplifier is used to increase the level of the electrical

signal from the sound source so that it can be heard at sufficient volume from the loudspeaker. Finally, the loudspeaker is the device that converts the electrical signal from the amplifier back into mechanical energy (sound).

In reality, we often need to amplify more than one source. Instead of using one amplifier and loudspeaker for each source, a mixer is used to mix the sources together so that only one amp and speaker can be used for all of them.

MICROPHONES

Transducers are devices that change one kind of energy (mechanical or electrical) into another. Microphones are transducers as they convert the mechanical energy of sound into electrical energy.

The vibrations in the air cause movements in a small diaphragm in the microphone. The diaphragm moves a coil in a magnetic field, which generates an electrical signal. As with an electric guitar, microphones produce a very low-level (weak) signal which needs an extra stage of amplification before it can be sent to a power amplifier. This extra stage is a special preamplifier, called a microphone preamp (or 'mic pre'), built into most PA mixers — but it also exists as a separate unit for special applications.

There are many microphones available for different applications, and entire books have been written about them, but the two important things you need to know are: the type of mic and its polar pattern.

Type

Two types of mic are used live: condenser and dynamic. Condensers have a better high-frequency response and are powered either by onboard batteries or remote power supplied by the mixing desk — called 'phantom' power. Dynamics are more rugged, require no power source and generally have a warmer sound.

Polar pattern

Polar pattern refers to the direction from which the mic picks up sound. In a PA, cardioid (unidirectional) mics are used, which pick up sound mostly from the front of the mic, a little from the sides and very little from behind the mic. An important fact is that the closer to a cardioid mic a source is, the more the bass response is boosted. This is called the 'proximity effect', and is the reason for vocals sounding warmer when the mic is held close to the mouth.

above *Mics are often geared for vocals, guitars or drums.*

Leads

In order to avoid hum and interference in microphones, 'balanced line' connections are used. This is a three-wire system consisting of positive ('hot'), negative (cold') and ground (earth) signals. The plugs are 3-pin XLR connectors, which come in male and female configurations. XLR to jack cables should be avoided as they defeat the balancing.

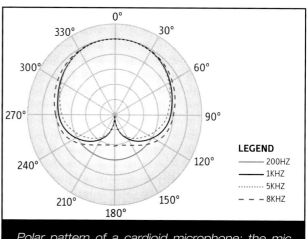

LEGEND
——— 200HZ
——— 1KHZ
.... 5KHZ
– – – 8KHZ

Polar pattern of a cardioid microphone: the mic faces toward 0°.

MIC'ING ELECTRIC GUITARS

While there are no hard and fast rules for microphone choice, dynamic microphones are usually used. Two models that are popular are the Shure SM57 and the Sennheiser MD421.

The most important factor in getting a great electric guitar sound is the sound that comes out of the amp — and this is determined by a combination of guitar, amp and player. With a multi-speaker amp, you will often find that one speaker is 'sweeter-sounding' than the others. This is the one to mic up. Set up the mic right against the amp's grille, pointing it directly into the speaker or at a slight angle from the outer rim of the speaker, pointing toward the centre.

Line-level sources

This refers to the group of devices with output at a suitable level to be connected straight into the mixer with no preamplification. Devices in this category include CD players, keyboards and amplifier line-outs.

AMPLIFIERS

As mentioned earlier, amplifiers take a line-level signal and boost it to the levels required to drive a loudspeaker. We refer to all these amplifiers as power amplifiers as they handle the high powers required to drive loudspeakers. Here are some of the facts you need to understand to ensure that the correct amp is chosen for your needs.

Power

When selecting an amplifier, output power is the main parameter needing attention. It is expressed in watts, e.g. 500 watts (500W). In the case of a two-channel amp (stereo), this is usually per channel. Care must be taken here as the power delivered by an amplifier depends on the impedance of the loudspeaker being driven by the amplifier. The wrong impedance can damage both.

top *A guitar amplifier is mic'ed up with the venerable Shure SM57 microphone.*

above *PA power amplifiers tend to be large and heavy, but are made to produce lots of power and take punishment.*

Impedance

Impedance is the measure of resistance offered by the loudspeaker, expressed in ohms. The higher the impedance of the speaker, the less power will be delivered by the amplifier. When reading the specification for an amplifier, the power will be given for a specific impedance, e.g. 500 watts into 4 ohms; 250 watts into 8 ohms. If only a single figure is stated, then assume this is for a 4-ohm load, which is the industry standard.

NOTE: **Do not drive an amp at lower than rated impedance!**

This can cause your amp and speakers to burn out. Most PA loudspeakers have a standardized 8-ohm load rating (although not all), which means you need to know a little about impedance to make sure you have the correct rating connected to your amp. Refer also to Chapter 3, p57 for more on connecting speakers to get the right impedance.

LOUDSPEAKERS

The loudspeaker is the final link in the chain. In essence it is a very simple device: a box or cabinet containing one or more drivers (speakers) that produce the actual sound.

Different combinations of drivers and cabinet construction methods produce speakers with different characteristics — some made for volume, others made for quality, and some even made for price. Below, we look at the components of a loudspeaker.

The cabinet

Basically a box in which the drivers are mounted, the cabinet plays an important part in the overall sound of the loudspeaker. It can be constructed from wood, fibreglass or plastic. An effort is made to use materials that are as rigid as possible so the cabinet doesn't start vibrating when the speaker is in use, as this affects the sound. In better cabinets this is aided by bracing (struts for structural reinforcement).

The way the cabinet is put together is also very important: dimensions, volume and construction tech-niques all affect the sound. Many cabinets have a hole, known as a 'port', that allows the air to move freely in and out of the cabinet as the driver cones move. This extends the bass response of the cabinet. Cabinet design can be very scientific these days, and is often computer assisted. A good design can make a cheaper set of drivers sound good, but the reverse is also true: a good set of speakers can sound terrible when slapped haphazardly into a chipboard box.

The drivers

Drivers — the components that produce the sounds — generally comprise a coil of wire sitting within a magnetic field. As electric current flows through the wire, it moves within the magnetic field. By attaching a diaphragm to the coil, we can make a volume of air move at the same time, producing sound waves.

A single driver can be capable of producing the full range of audible sounds (i.e. you do get 'full range' drivers in the smaller sizes). In practice, however, multiple drivers are more common in a loudspeaker for efficiency. A two-way system would have a low to midrange frequency driver and a high-frequency driver too. One of the reasons for separating these out is that high frequencies are more directional.

High-frequency drivers are normally mounted along with a 'horn' in order to control the direction of the frequency, or sound. If you take a look at the specification for a loudspeaker, you should find a dispersion property; this indicates the angle at which the high frequencies leave the loudspeaker. Narrower dispersion angles (30–60°) are more suited to what is termed 'long-throw' speaker applications (where your audience is further away) whereas wider angles (90–100°) are better for 'short-throw' applications (where the audience is closer).

Crossovers

When a loudspeaker has more than one driver, we need a way to split the frequencies so that the low frequencies go to the low-frequency driver and the high frequencies to their corresponding driver, and so on. This is done using a crossover, which splits an incoming audio signal into its component frequency bands. Most two-way or three-way loudspeakers have a built-in crossover network that does this job. It is known as a 'passive' crossover (as it needs no additional power).

More advanced systems use an external crossover termed an 'active' crossover. It works slightly differently as it is inserted before the amplifier. In this case,

you will require additional amplifier channels to run each individual driver. The technique is referred to as bi-amping or tri-amping (depending on whether the sound is split into two or three frequencies).

Such systems tend to sound cleaner, more detailed and controlled, with each driver being run by its own dedicated amplifier channel. The downside is the expense, since more amplifiers are required as well as the active crossover.

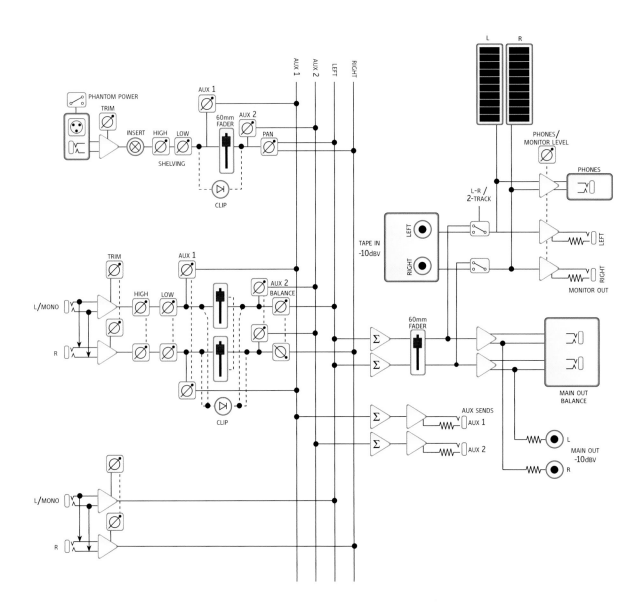

THE MIXER

In its simplest form a mixer takes several input signals and combines them into a single output. To allow a little more control, individual level (volume) controls are fitted to the inputs and a master level control to the output. This then allows not only control of the overall output level from the unit but also the balance between the individual inputs. Most mixers have more functionality than this and these extra functions are needed when setting up a PA system.

All mixers have the same basic function: they combine and control the volume of a number of inputs, add effects and route the signal to a variety of destinations. In a live sound setup, these destinations will usually be power amps and speakers.

The key to understanding mixers (whether specific models or mixers in general) is to look at the block diagram — that is, the graphic representation of the different sections of the mixer. This shows you how they are connected to each other and the paths that the signal can take. The illustration (opposite) is a simple block diagram of a four-channel mixer. It shows the two main sections of a mixer: the channel strip (one for each input) and the master section, which combines all the channel strips and sets all output options.

The channel strip

Mixers have what are known as channel strips, a row of controls that are dedicated to one input.

THE INPUTS

A mixer has two types of input. Line level is for instruments that have a powerful output signal, such as synthesizers; this is usually an unbalanced 6mm (¼in) phone jack socket. A microphone input is a balanced XLR (3-pin) socket for the relatively low signal level from mics. Balanced line-level signals are also connected here, with the mic preamp's gain control turned down.

below *This is a large 32-channel, 8-group, 2-bus Yamaha mixing desk with all of the features needed for mixing a moderately sized band.*

MICROPHONE PREAMP

This is the most important component in the mixer. Mics produce quite a low voltage, so they need a lot of boosting to reach a level that the mixer can work with. This needs to be done with as low noise and distortion as possible, because if the signal quality is degraded at this point in the mixer, the noise will only be compounded by everything that comes later in the signal path. Therefore the quality of the preamps has to be very high. Trim or gain controls on the preamp section are used to set the level of the signal entering the channel strip. This is essential to ensure that the signal-to-noise ratio (the amount of noise generated) by the channel is kept to a minimum.

Better mixers will often have a low-cut switch on the mic preamp. When engaged, this will cut all frequencies below a certain point (usually 80Hz). It is used to remove the very low frequencies on the instruments that do not need them (usually everything apart from the bass guitar and kick drum mic), preventing a bass build-up in the system. A bass build-up will use a lot of the power of your amplification for no purpose and will 'muddy' the sound.

Your mic preamps may also have a switch for phantom power, which is used to send 48V of power down the mic cable to drive condenser mics. While this feature will be

available on every mic channel of the mixer, it will often be turned on for all mic channels via a single switch. Don't worry if you have a mix of condenser and dynamic mics; any modern dynamic mic will 'ignore' phantom power. However, be aware that badly designed equipment can object to, or be destroyed by, phantom power.

INSERTS

Inserts allow you to insert effects such as equalizers (EQ) and compressors into the signal path of the channel strip. Inserts can also be used to send the signal to another mixing desk (for advanced monitoring applications) or multitrack recorder (for multitrack recording of live performances without any EQ or effects).

EQUALIZATION

The tonal adjustment section of the strip, this will usually be in the form of a two- or three-band EQ (low, mid, high frequencies).

Better mixers often have a 'parametric' EQ for the midrange (or even two!). This has an extra control (usually called 'frequency') which allows you to 'tune' the midrange to the desired frequency. You can also find the exact frequency causing a problem (e.g. feedback or an odd tone) and fix it.

left *All the controls on this mixer's channel strip are for one input only.*

A live sound engineer at work with an impressive mixing console that is supporting a large band performing on stage.

FADER

The fader is where you set the level of the channel, that is, the volume you want in the mix. Try to have the fader set somewhere around the 0dB mark or lower (usually marked clearly on the mixer). This gives you some 'headroom' to push the channel higher when needed (for solos, etc.). By setting it at a higher level, you can introduce unnecessary noise to the signal.

If the set level is not sufficient to make the instrument loud enough without having to push it higher than this point, check your input gain/trim control.

AUXILIARY (AUX.) SENDS

This is where things start getting interesting. An 'auxiliary send' (aux.) allows you to send a copy of the channel signal somewhere else, often combining it with other channels to a separate output. Why? It allows you, for example, to send a different mix to a monitor system or add effects to some of the channels but not others. There are two options: pre- and post-fade. A pre-fader is what you will usually use for monitoring; the signal is taken before the fader changes the level (often before the EQ, too; check your mixer's block diagram).

The reason for using pre-fade aux. sends is that, as you mix — changing the level of an instrument in the main mix — using the fader, the volume of the instrument remains constant in the monitors, keeping the musician happy.

Post-fade is used for effect send: as you bring down the level of an instrument, the effect level also diminishes. It is nice but not essential for a mixer to give you the option of changing an aux. send from pre- to post-fade. Some mixers have the sends preconfigured as pre- or post-send, calling them 'monitor' and 'effects' respectively.

PAN POT

A 'pan pot' (from 'panoramic potentiometer') positions the sound of the instrument in a stereo mix. Usually, for live sound, everything in the mix is positioned in the middle (mono), so that people standing in different spots will hear the same mix.

Even if you are doing a stereo mix, it is better to keep your bassier instruments in the middle. This shares the load of the bass end between the two channels of your power amps; human hearing tends to perceive any frequencies below +/-250Hz in the centre, regardless of the source direction.

OTHER CONTROLS/SWITCHES

Your mixer may have some controls or switches not covered above. In short:

Group (or bus) routing: lets you choose a pair of groups to which to send the output of the channel. (See routing.)
Mute switches: for turning off a channel completely; also to mute mics not in use for a particular song.

Solo switches: the opposite of a mute switch, these switch off all the channels that are not soloed; for setting trim levels and hearing one track in isolation.
High pass filter switch: this is the same as a low-cut switch.
Pad: cuts down the level of excessively loud input signals at the input.
Phase reverse: swaps the polarity of the input to cure some multiple mic'ing problems.

THE MASTER SECTION

This serves to combine all the channel strips and set all output options (see the photograph opposite). It is important to consult your mixer's manual for the block diagram of your specific mixer. You will find that any additional features are easier to understand once you have understood the basic functions featured here. Detailed explanations of each of the 'blocks' are given in the text below.

Input routing & mixing

This is where all the incoming signals are mixed and sent to various outputs. The incoming signals can be channel strip outputs or auxiliary returns from effect units, etc. Basically, this section allows you to define a number of sub-mixes, called groups (although to confuse things, both groups and buses are simply called 'buses' by some. For the purposes of this explanation, they are named 'groups'. Each group is a (usually stereo) sub-mix with its own separate faders.

The purpose is to assign all the drum tracks to one group, guitars to another, vocals to a third, and so on. The level of each group can then be changed with only one or two faders. Instead of juggling, for instance, five drum tracks, four vocals, one bass and two guitars — a total of 12 faders — you have only four groups that must be controlled.

Output groups

As discussed above, each of these is a (usually stereo) sub-mix with its own separate faders.

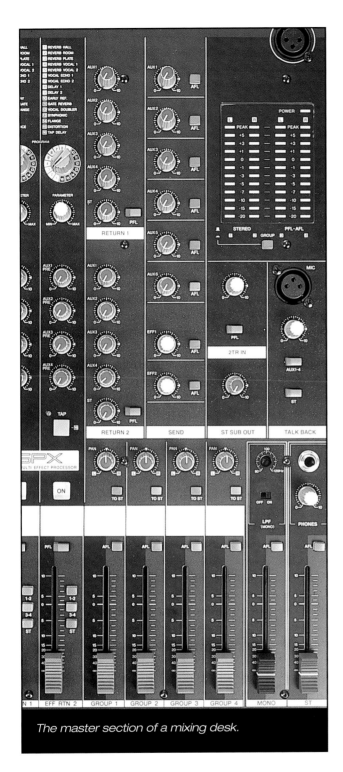

The master section of a mixing desk.

Group routing & mixing

If you have eight groups on your mixer but only one or two power amps and pairs of speakers, you obviously need to mix the groups together into an even smaller number of outputs (buses). Once again, like groups, buses are usually stereo pairs with their own faders.

Inserts

As with channel inserts, output bus inserts allow you to 'insert' effects such as equalizers into the signal path, before the outputs.

How many in a mixer?

Manufacturers will usually give you a number like 32:8:2 or 16:4:2 or even just 16:2. In the first two cases, the first figure is the number of input channels, the second is the number of groups, and the third is output buses. In the latter case there are no groups, so the middle number is missing — signifying a simple 16-channel to 2-channel (stereo) mixer. With really complex mixers you may even find a figure like 64:16:8:2. This tells you that there are two layers of groups.

Often these numbers will form part of the model number. For instance: the Mackie 1604 is a 16-channel, 4-bus desk and the Behringer 3282 is a 32-channel, 8-group, 2-bus desk.

MONITOR SYSTEMS

A monitor system is a separate but connected PA system that allows musicians to hear themselves and their band mates. Some musical sounds — the voice being a prime example — are relatively quiet in comparison to those of a lot of modern amplified, and some acoustic, instruments. While these quieter sources may be amplified by the PA system, the PA speakers should be in front of the musicians, pointing away from them.

Some instruments — particularly horns — are directional, and throw most of their sound forward with very little moving backward to any musicians behind the horns. A monitor system allows these instruments to be amplified so that the sound is sent to on-stage musicians, allowing all musicians to hear one another.

Another problem a monitor system helps overcome is delayed sound. Sound takes approximately three milliseconds (3ms) to travel 1m (3ft) — that is, about 0.3m/1ft per ms. While this seems fast for most purposes, consider that two musicians on opposite sides

Monitor speakers allow musicians on stage to hear themselves and their band mates clearly.

of a 10m-wide (33ft) stage will be hearing each other 30ms later. This is an appreciable delay when the two musicians are trying to play in time with each other.

Also, in the example of a vocalist singing with a band in a large venue (with about 25m/80ft from the stage to the back wall), the delay is the time it takes for the amplified sound to travel to the rear wall and back to the stage again: that is, a total of 50m (165ft) and 150ms late.

COMPONENTS OF A MONITOR SYSTEM
Output

For most purposes, it is a simple system. The first thing you need is for your mixing desk to have at least one extra output to send a signal to the monitors. Most mixing desks designed for live sound have a dedicated monitor output and a send control on each input channel. This allows you to send as much or as little of each input as you need to the monitors, effectively sending a different mix to the musicians.

An aux. send does exactly the same thing, but will often give you the option to send the signal as a pre-fade or a post-fade (before or after the main faders). Monitor systems should be pre-fade, so that changes made to the main mix will not affect the monitor mix. Post-fade is usually used as an effect send. If your mixer does not have monitor or aux. sends, there is often a second output for the main mix and this can be used if need be, although it will not allow you to have a separate monitor mix.

Amplifier

The next stage in your monitor system is the amplifier, usually a single channel for each monitor mix. A two-channel amp is often used to send two different monitor mixes.

Your drummer, for instance, may want a monitor mix that is predominantly bass guitar, while your vocalist may want a mix that is mostly vocal (I speak from experience!). Depending on how many free aux. sends, amps and speakers you have, you can have as many separate monitor mixes. Most PA amps are 4 ohms, which means you can slave two 8-ohm monitor speakers from each channel. This means that a single twin-channel amp can drive four monitor cabinets with two different monitor mixes.

Monitor cabinet

The third and final piece of the puzzle is the monitor cabinet (speakers and box). These are the wedge-shaped speaker boxes at the musicians' feet.

They are made this way for two reasons: to be unobtrusive to the audience and to project the sound in such a way that the on-stage mics are less likely to pick up the sound from them, thus avoiding feedback. Some monitor cabinets are 'active', that is, they have an amplifier built into them. Active cabinets usually have an output

for one 'slave' cabinet, which allows you to connect one 'passive' (unamplified) monitor to them.

PLACEMENT AND TIPS

* Monitors should, where possible, be on the floor in front of the microphones, facing the back of the stage. This helps avoid feedback as their sound projects along the axis of the mic where it is the least sensitive.
* Make a point of getting the best monitor cabinets you can afford, as a bad quality sound will affect your performance.
* If you have a band member who keeps raising the volume on his (her) amp or instrument, it's a sure sign he cannot hear himself properly and needs more level in the monitor mix.
* Drummers usually want to hear the bass guitar; bassists need to hear the kick drum. You will find that on a concrete floor, the musicians need more kick in the monitor mix than they do on a wooden stage (as they cannot feel the pulse as well). Many vocalists and guitarists want mostly their own sound in the monitors.

Wireless In-ear Monitors

These are becoming popular as they totally eliminate the problem of feedback and clear the stage area of large monitor speakers and cables. They consist of :
* an in-ear monitor, which looks something like a hearing aid or pair of in-ear headphones; it serves to both play the sound of the monitor mix and to block out outside stage noise, which interferes with the monitor mix
* a radio receiver worn by the musician, which receives the monitor mix via radio and sends it to the in-ear monitor
* a transmitter, which broadcasts the monitor mix from the mixing desk; can be multichannel to send multiple monitor mixes on different radio frequencies.

CHAPTER 8

In the STUDIO

At some point you may end up in a recording studio. It might be to record your band's first demo CD or it might be as a session guitarist. With any luck you may have worked extensively in a home recording studio beforehand and will have a good idea of what to expect from some elements of the recording process. For the majority of first-time studio guitarists, the difference between studio and live playing can be a bit of a shock.

Once you've decided to record a demo or a CD, think of it as a major project and be prepared. The most important thing is to make sure you understand all the aspects of your project.

You want a good quality recording without spending too much money. Where do you start? While you cannot avoid spending money, there are ways to maximize the results you're getting. Choosing the best studio for your project

The live room of a recording studio should have a pleasing sound and some natural reverb. The majority of a band's instruments will be recorded in this room.

and planning your recording session is key to a great product. It speaks for your talent, the work done by your recording engineer and the studio. Although it takes quite some effort and patience, it will pay off in the end, so do your homework!

DIFFERENCES BETWEEN STUDIO AND STAGE

What works on the gig doesn't always work in the studio. The emphasis in the studio is on your playing and your sound. It is a very critical listening environment in

left *The difference between recording in the studio and playing live can be unsettling for new recording musicians.*

which any flaw, regardless how small, is obvious. On stage you can often get away with errors due to the atmosphere and 'feel' of a live performance; in the studio, errors are immediately and glaringly apparent. Studio work is very exacting, requiring a thorough control of your instrument, sensitivity to musical demands and great patience.

In many cases, you will be isolated from the other performers, sometimes merely by screens, but often in a totally different room. You might even record your parts on a different day! It's possible you will need to record using headphones, with the majority of your monitor sound coming from them. Your sound will often be drier, with less effects, to make sure that your timing is more accurate.

CHOOSING A STUDIO

When it comes to making any recording, the studio plays a creative role. Every recording studio is different and you need to choose one that is comfortable for you to work in, will suit your budget and has the equipment and staff to meet all your recording needs. You also need to consider the kind of facilities you will need to recreate your sound on record, based on the type of music you make, before you start looking.

Your budget

The cost of the studio will probably be the first criterium in your budget. If you have a contract with a major label, it's expected of you to do the best job possible — and they provide the finance for this. You need to use fairly expensive major recording and mastering facilities, but the budget becomes less of an issue. However, don't go overboard, as the expense comes out of royalties at the end of the day!

If, on the other hand, you are an unsigned band financing your first studio outing, the decision on where to record inevitably comes down to money. In this situation, you will have to accept that almost any session organized on a small budget necessitates some compromises. With this in mind, work out how much you can afford and then shop around. But do remember, when you're putting a lot of effort into making a recording, saving some money at the cost of good quality is the last thing you want to do.

Always split your recording budget, reserving at least 25 per cent for mixing and mastering. The bulk is for studio time. It will always take longer to record than you expect, and watching the clock may have disastrous results on your music. So planning at this stage is imperative.

It's better to go for a project deal instead of number of hours. Studios may do a special deal for a 'block' booking, where you book the studio exclusively for a consecutive number of days. If your schedule is well-planned, it means you can set up your gear and leave it that way for the duration of the recording — which saves time.

Finding a studio

There are various ways to source a studio: the Internet, yellow pages of your telephone directory and advertisements in music publications. The best way is to find out from other bands who play your style of music where they have made their recordings. If you have heard another band's recording and like the sound, find out where they made it.

Try to find one studio that's not too far from your location; having to undertake a long drive before recording doesn't help the performance and adds to the cost. Once you have a list of studios that fit with your budget, go and take a look at them.

The control room of a recording studio, where the engineer sits, should sound quite 'dead' and very neutral, with very little reverb.

THE STUDIO ENVIRONMENT
Atmosphere

It's pretty important to feel comfortable and confident in the studio, especially when you're recording. Do you like what you see and hear, and does the studio have a pleasant and creative environment?

The gear

A professional recording studio will offer a comprehensive list of equipment and services. It should have at least 16-track capability, a decent selection of microphones, microphone preamps, compressors and other effects processors. If the studio is using a computer-based recording system, find out what plug-in effects are offered in the system. While studio equipment is important, beware of impressive lists. A studio with a long list of top-of-the-line gear will almost certainly be more expensive and, in the end, you may use less than half of them. On the other hand, it should have enough equipment for you not to be limited when it comes to mixdown.

Vocal tracks are generally recorded in a small isolation booth, where the quality of the sound is of the utmost importance.

Control room

A good studio control room should have a neutral playback system and acoustics that give an honest representation of the mix. It's no help if your recording sounds good in the studio but nowhere else. It's a good idea to take home a copy of a section mixed in the studio to listen to on your car and home stereos.

The sound

Every studio has a distinctive 'sound' which comes from the particular acoustic spaces and combinations of equipment it contains. It is standard practice for an

engineer or studio to have examples of their work to give to prospective clients. Take a listen to tracks that are in a similar style to yours to gauge whether the sound is one that you like.

Live room

This is where the recording of the majority of the instruments takes place. It should be a quiet, good-sounding environment, preferably capable of recording several instruments at once with some degree of isolation. There should be screens to place between the players to help with this.

Isolation room

This is a small room where vocals and other instruments that need a high degree of isolation are gen-

In the studio you rely on the recording engineer, so it's important that he understands your music and you get along with him.

erally recorded. Its sound should be suitable for singing, and the room should not be too small in the event that your vocalist suffers from claustrophobia!

The engineer

More than anything else, you need to have confidence in the people you're working with. The most important of these is the engineer — who will bring to bear his ears and experience. In the end, the most impressive equipment will only sound as good as the engineer's ability to use it.

Talk to the engineer and see if he (or she) is sympathetic to your music; make sure it's someone you'll get along with. You also should find the opportunity to hear several different examples of the engineer's previous work to determine if he is well suited to

recording and mixing your type of music. This is probably the single most important decision you will make in planning your session.

Once you've chosen your engineer, make sure he hears your band so that he can get an idea of what you sound like. Invite him to a few gigs or make a basic recording with a tape recorder to which he can listen. This means that when you get into the studio, the engineer will already have an idea of how to approach things. You need to be aware, however, that an engineer who is in demand may not have the time to attend your gig.

PREPARING FOR RECORDING

Some of the most important factors in producing a professional-sounding recording are dependent on the preparation that takes place before you even enter the studio. Recording can be a very inspiring and enjoyable experience but can quickly become stressful. If you are not relaxed when you're recording your material, you'll be left with a recording you know could have been better. Time is always money, and in the studio environment, time is always lots of money. The better prepared you are, the quicker you will finish and the less it will cost.

Selecting your songs

Choosing which songs to record can be a difficult decision to make if you have a large selection. You probably won't have the time or money to record all of your

Personal Preparation

Know the arrangements backward

You need to know your parts really well. Although it's easy to think you already do, in the studio you may be recording your parts with very few instruments already recorded, and you might find that when playing live, you are getting your cues from other instruments — or even visual cues. In the studio those cues are suddenly not there, and you will find you don't know when the changes are.

Your sounds

Make sure you know how to get good basic sounds for each song. Experiment with different sounds until you find the one you think fits best, then make sure you know how to recreate it. Avoid reverb and delay effects, as well as any nonessential effects, as these are best done in the studio with the professional effects they have there.

Practice

Practise your timing and technique; work with a metronome or drum box to make sure your timing is spot-on. If you have to do multiple takes of your guitar part while recording, it will become harder and harder to get it right until you are forced to come back and do it after some rest — which wastes a lot of time. Make sure beforehand that you can execute your parts without buzzes, finger squeaks, and so on.

Your equipment

Make sure your strings are new. It's easy for an engineer to tame the treble a bit if they are too bright, but it's not the same to add treble electronically where there is none to begin with. However, don't put a new set on the same day you are due to record; give them a day or two to settle.

Ensure that your guitar is set up properly so that the frets or pick-ups don't buzz and your guitar sounds the best it can. The same applies to your amps, leads and pedals. Make sure there is no electrical buzz off them and that the only noise is that being made by you and your guitar!

Pack spares of absolutely everything. If you use batteries in your pedal effects, take two or three spares along. If you have active pick-ups, put a new battery in your guitar and take a spare for that too. Take along at least one spare set of strings, a handful of plectrums and even a few leads — as well as anything else you generally use to play.

songs, so you have to decide which ones are the strongest and best represent you. Ask friends or regular audience members which tracks they like the most and which ones they would like to hear recorded. More often than not, there will be some common songs in everybody's answer.

Preparing your songs

Before anything else, make sure all your songs are completely written, discussed, and rehearsed before you enter the studio. What you don't want is to be using costly studio time to work out things that should have been done beforehand.

You need to be sure of the arrangements, harmonies, and so on within your songs. It is important to set the tempo of all your songs before entering the studio. Make sure to practise with a 'click track' — the studio equivalent of a metronome, which plays in your headphones. It's entirely possible that you will be asked to do so in the studio (especially if the band's timing is not perfect), and it is something which takes a little getting used to.

A good idea when preparing your songs is to make recordings at your rehearsals. This allows you to listen back and give some thought as to how they could be improved.

RECORDING DAY

Get plenty of sleep the night before. On recording day wear something comfortable and take a sweater along too. Bring gloves in case you need to keep your hands

right *It is crucial that you are well prepared before entering the studio and the meter starts running.*

warm between takes. If you have long hair, tie it back or ensure it is kept out of your face. Don't wear anything that's noisy when you move around — for example, bracelets, necklaces, other jewellery, stiff clothing, and so on.

THE RECORDING PROCESS

Even though, as a musician, you may not be operating the knobs and faders, a working knowledge of the operations involved in recording helps to give you some measure of control.

Setting up

If you're recording together as a band, arrive at the studio together and on time. It's your money that is being spent, even if for the moment a record company is picking up the bill.

For recording sessions where a large drum kit needs to be set up, try to arrange for the drummer to come in a day early, or earlier on the

Setting up and recording the drums can be one of the most time-consuming aspects of the recording process, but it happens to be one of the most crucial.

Backing tracks

Recording each instrument separately is best soundwise because this provides control of the individual sounds. This doesn't mean that a band will not play together — the most important thing is to capture a great performance. But generally, the recording will be done in stages whenever possible.

It is usual to first record the drums, bass and possibly one other rhythm instrument 'live' at the same time. If necessary, the vocalist can sing a 'scratch track' to guide the rhythm section through the song; band members will be in the isolation room and the vocals will be sent through headphones to the band. Playing with headphones on for the first time can be a strange experience, but it is usually necessary. The vocalist must be prepared to do as many takes as necessary to get an acceptable performance from the band. This guide vocal will usually be replaced after everything else is recorded, unless it is better than everything else recorded later — which sometimes does happen!

Some bands prefer to record all the instruments in one go, doing repeated takes until the right combination of accuracy and excitement blend together. This can take some time though, so be prepared to take breaks to keep fresh.

You might prefer to put down guide drums from a drum machine and build the full track with the other instruments first. The drummer will then record later on in the process when the track is more complete. This can give the final track a better feel, but it does require that the drummer follow the timing rather than the other way around.

Always listen to what you've recorded. You don't want to discover problems when the engineer does

appointed day, to set up the kit. The rest of the band can set up around the kit if this is how they like to work. Isolation screens can be placed around the drums to prevent 'spill' from other instruments reaching the drum microphones. Alternatively, the other band members can play in the control or isolation rooms, leaving the drummer alone in the live room. There are no preset rules about this: do whatever feels most comfortable.

Mic'ing up

With most instruments, mic'ing up is as vital a part of the recording process as actually playing the notes themselves. Many engineers have their own pet instrument, amplifier and microphone combinations, but what works for one player (or song!) does not necessarily work for the next. Your engineer will want to experiment with mic placement and different microphones. This will need some patience on your part, as it can be time-consuming. However, it is a critical part of the recording process, and more time spent here will ensure a better result.

the mixing and have to come back for more recording. This not only adds to the cost, but it will be extremely difficult to get the same sound again.

Overdubs

After the rhythm tracks are finished, the other instrumental 'overdubs' are added, one at a time. These are usually additional support instruments, solos, and so on. The main restriction on this is the number of available tracks left on the recorder, but unless you are in a 12-track (or less) studio, this should not be a problem. And just because there are tracks to spare doesn't mean you have to use them all — sometimes a simpler arrangement works better.

At this point if budget allows, extra session musicians can also be brought in to add parts to improve the track. It could be an instrument the band members don't play but the producer has decided should be part of the song. It could also be replacing a synthesized part with the real instrument (like strings), as this often makes a difference to the quality of the recording. It is also common at this stage for the producer to arrange for high-quality sampled parts.

Vocals

Finally, the track is ready for lead vocals, and eventually, background vocal parts. This can be the most demanding time of all as the artist has to be relaxed to deliver a special performance.

The most satisfying way of dealing with a lead vocal is to get one magic take that can't be faulted. However, one of the best ways to capture a great lead vocal part is to do what is commonly called 'comping' (composite track). The idea is to have the lead vocalist sing several complete vocal per-

formances from start to finish, and record them on different tracks. Then the best parts of each take are mixed into one seamless performance. Background vocals can also benefit from this technique by having one good chorus section performed, then simply copying and pasting to subsequent choruses.

Mixing

Mixing is the process of putting everything together and achieving a great balance. All the instruments have to be heard properly, and they need to complement each other.

This sounds simple, but is actually complicated as every instrument carries a different energy in varying frequencies and these have to be equalized so they don't interfere with each other. Each sound has to be placed in space — both stereo and depth while the voices or leads have to stand out.

In a high-budget recording it is possible that another, different studio will be used for mixdown. Some studios offer computerized mixing desks which store

above *Getting used to using headphones and using a click track can be an unexpected adjustment when recording for the first time.*

Mixing by committee is not advisable. Rather allow one band member to work with the engineer.

fader positions in memory and move them during a complex mix. During recording, these facilities are of limited use and also tend to be expensive, so in this instance a cheaper, nonautomated studio is best.

SOME TIPS:

- Allow at least a couple of days between the recording and the mixing, as this helps you gain some objectivity and gives your ears a rest. Get the engineer to do a rough mix of the songs for you to listen to in the meantime; this will give you a good idea of what needs to be done to create a good mix.
- Designate one band member to help with the mixing – mixing 'by committee' is not a good idea.
- Take each mix home overnight to listen to on a familiar sound system before deciding on a final mix.

HOME STUDIOS

Another more recent alternative to buying studio time is to finance your own studio. The advances in computer technology have made the Digital Audio Workstation (DAW) – a computer dedicated to music production – affordable and very powerful. If you can afford two or three days' recording time at a reasonably cheap studio, you could probably buy enough basic equipment to turn your computer into a DAW. This offers a number of advantages. Your studio time suddenly costs nothing and you can record for as long as you like, when you like, or spend extra time re-arranging a song at the last minute.

There is a wide variety of recording software to choose from, such as Cakewalk's Sonar, Steinberg's Cubase and many others.

There has also been an explosion of software synthesizers, which model vintage synthesizers and samplers and also make some new and radical departures from the norm. 'Plug-in' effects – software effect processors — are numerous and you will find many already packaged with your recording software.

All-in-one studio hard-disk recorders are also quite popular. These have everything aside from microphones and cables built into one unit. They are ideal for cyberphobes as they offer a relatively simple method for musicians to record, avoiding software and hardware conflicts.

The downside with either software or hardware recorders is that you have to be your own engineer. This is a steep learning curve for most musicians, with every new piece of technology needing knowledge to operate it, and even more to master it. There is a real danger of you becoming more engineer than musician as the technology takes up more of your time.

Things like good monitors, mics and mic preamps cost money, so it can get very expensive as you gradually upgrade. You might want to start a partnership with another musician or engineer friend to buy more equipment and expand the system.

While some hit recordings have been made in the home studio, it is still not a replacement for a professional facility with experienced and dedicated staff, and a cupboard full of microphones, each costing more than your car! Unless you have lots of time and money, though, rather use it more as a demo studio.

RECORDING YOUR ELECTRIC GUITAR AT HOME

An electric guitar is capable of a wide range of sounds and is unique in that the amplification used adds to the texture of the sound. The single most important detail in getting great electric guitar sounds is that the sound coming out of the amp should be great. This is determined by the guitar, the amp and speakers – and the person playing it!

Guitar setup

As with the tips earlier in this chapter, make sure the guitar is free from buzzes and rattles, the strings are relatively new and the intonation is set properly.

Mic'ing up

It is important to remember that from a recording viewpoint, the amp and speakers are part of the instrument and should be treated as such. Open-backed guitar cabinets emit sound from both the front and the rear of the cabinet, and you must often capture both to reproduce the real sound of the amp. The key to getting a great guitar sound is to constantly experiment and apply some basic physics.

Usually a guitar amp is mic'ed with a close-up and with a distant room microphone or two. This gives you a range of sounds to experiment with.

In the smaller home studio, or those studios with an unflattering room sound, you may want to omit using the room microphone.

If you do use a room mic, take time to find a spot in the room where the amp sounds good and a second spot distant from the amp that also gives out a good sound. Your hearing is the most sophisticated measuring instrument, so walk around the room looking for 'sweet' spots; you'll know them when you find them. You will need to experiment: try different mics; move them closer and farther; test different angles; try putting the amp in a corner, on a concrete floor, on a wood floor — there are many options!

The dynamic SM57 microphone is the workhorse of the recording studio.

Close mic

This will usually be a dynamic mic such as a Shure SM57 or a Sennheiser MD421. Both can handle the volume levels and have enough frequency range to cope with the limited response of an electric guitar.

Set up the mic right against the amp's grill cloth, pointing it at a slight angle from the outer rim of the speaker toward the centre. Moving the mic toward the side will result in a mellower sound, as will moving the mic away from the cloth. The close mic gives a dry, powerful, detailed sound.

A software compressor: compressors should be used in moderation when close-mic'ing a guitar amp.

MULTI-SPEAKER CABINETS

If you use a multi-speaker guitar cabinet, one of the speakers will have a better sound than the others. This is the one you designate for the close mic.

If you don't already know which one it is, spend some time playing with the amp and listening to it to figure it out. There is nothing to gain by mic'ing more than one speaker.

Room mic

For the room mic, place a condenser microphone anywhere from ½–2m (1½–6½ft) in front of the amp (at the same height as the amp) and point the mic at one of the speakers. The further it is from the amp, the more bass and less midrange it will have. More room sound will be picked up, making the sound bigger.

If you have enough tracks on your recorder, print the two mics to separate tracks so you are able to decide the balance between them later. If your track real estate is limited, mix them to the desired balance when recording to a single track; just be careful not to add in too much room mic, as you will not be able to change this later without re-recording.

Compression

If you have a compressor, you may want to use compression on the close mic. Set the compressor at a 3:1 ratio and adjust the threshold so that the compressor is usually working but is not squashing the signal too much.

Equalization

The electric guitar is not a natural instrument, so the only equalization rule is: get the sound you want. Adding 100–250Hz will give you more 'bottom'; rolling off 300–500Hz will eliminate some of the nasal quality; adding 700Hz will create a throaty or woody sound; taking it up to 1kHz (kilohertz) will give the guitar more edge; increasing to 3kHz will give the guitar more bite; and up to 5, 8, or 10kHz will make the sound brighter.

Doubling guitar parts

'Doubling' (playing the same part twice, on separate occasions and combining the sound) a rhythm guitar and panning (placing in stereo) the two tracks hard left and right can make the guitars sound huge — but consider what works best for the song. Is the rhythm

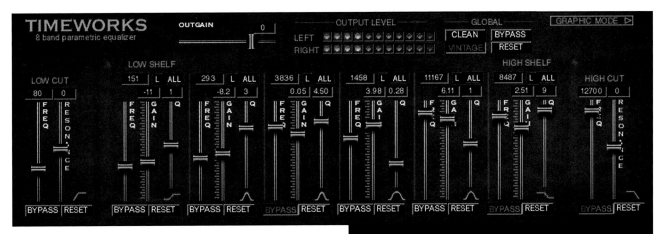

A software equalizer is used to ensure that each guitar track takes up a different area of the frequency spectrum.

guitar the featured instrument, or will there be several other guitars competing for space in the stereo spread? Sometimes less is more.

If you do decide to double the guitar, think about altering the sound on the double track to give you more thickness. You can change guitars and keep the amp the same, or vice versa. Change pick-up settings if using the same guitar on the second track. Equalize the two tracks differently ('scoop' mids out — i.e. reduce or diminish — from one and boost the bass and treble, then do the inverse for the second guitar).

Make sure the performance is really tight though, matching the first track's phrasing. Otherwise you might end up with a cluttered mix that would be better off with only one track of guitar.

Mixing

Start with the close mic; this should comprise the bulk of your guitar sound. If it sounds good as it is, don't add any room mic. For a slightly more distant but fuller sound, bring up the fader on the room mic. Slowly add that signal to the close sound. You'll have the detail of the close mic, but with the fullness that comes with

adding some 'room' sound to it. You don't need to mix the guitar much louder than the other instruments to make it sound big. It's how well you record it to begin with — if you've done that right you'll be in great shape for the mix.

Cakewalk Sonar Console: this is where the mix is made. To make it easier to use, it is laid out in a similar fashion to a hardware mixer.

CHAPTER 9

Guitar LEGENDS

There have been many illustrious names in the history of the electric guitar, and young players are constantly pushing the boundaries of possibility. This chapter profiles 35 innovative players who have blazed new pathways in technique, style or approach. Each entry lists the guitars generally used by the artist, as well as amplification, pedals and rack effects. Each entry includes a selection of key tracks and some recommended viewing. Naturally it is impossible to list every significant player, but the selection presented here covers a pretty fair slice of rock history.

CHET ATKINS

Chet Atkins once said that all he ever wanted to be was a famous guitarist. If that were all he had accomplished in his 77 years, it would have been enough. Without Chet Atkins, country music might never have crossed over into the pop charts. He helped create the poppy 'Nashville sound' and discovered and worked with many of the greatest artists of his time, as well as recording numerous solo records.

Atkins began his musical career on the fiddle. However, so attracted was he to the guitar that, at the age of nine, he traded a toy pistol for a guitar. Atkins mastered his instrument quickly, becoming an accomplished player by the time he left high school in 1941. He taught himself to fingerpick by listening to all kinds of music, and expanded Merle Travis's signature syncopated thumb and fingers roll, taking it into new territory.

In 1946 Atkins made his first appearance at Nashville's famed Grand Ole Opry, made his first records and began making regular performances on radio. He soon began working for radio stations, and in the 1950s when recording studios started opening up in Nashville, joined RCA Records. While he started as a session guitarist and a solo artist, he later worked as A&R man and producer. Eventually he ran the country music division of RCA. During his 15 years with RCA, he would typically put out two of his own albums and produce 30 other artists each year. Many of the biggest artists of the era were acts that Atkins either signed or produced.

During his later years Atkins departed from his traditional country roots, exploring a more contemporary style of instrumental music, demonstrating that he was a bold and tasteful jazz guitarist as well as a country picker. He did return to country on occasion, particularly on duet albums with Mark Knopfler and Jerry Reed.

left *Carlos Santana, shown on stage in Australia in 2003, electrifies audiences with his fiery, Latin-influenced playing.*

GEAR
Guitars: Gretsch Country Gentleman, Gibson Chet Atkins, Gibson Country Gentleman
Amps: Standel 25L15, Gretsch amplifiers

ESSENTIAL LISTENING
Me & Chet/Me & Jerry – Jerry Reed, Chet Atkins, 1998 • *The Essential Chet Atkins* – Chet Atkins, 1996 • *Neck & Neck* – Chet Atkins, Mark Knopfler, 1990

ESSENTIAL VIEWING
Rare Performances 1976–95 (Chet Atkins, 2002)

JEFF BECK

Hailed by many as the greatest virtuoso rock guitarist, Jeff Beck's career stretches from the early days of the British Invasion right up to the present. Beck was the guitarist who often pioneered techniques or styles that other guitarists made famous; even Hendrix admitted to using techniques he had seen Jeff Beck use.

An early experimenter with feedback and distortion, Beck was getting session work from Jimmy Page in the early 1960s, influencing other studio guitarists, such as Ritchie Blackmore of Deep Purple, with his wildly experimental style. He joined the bluesy Yardbirds in 1965 following Eric Clapton's departure.

Jeff then formed his own band, The Jeff Beck Group, and their 1968 debut *Truth* was a precursor to the heavy guitar rock that would follow in the coming years. His albums *Blow by Blow* and *Wired*, with synthesizer wizard Jan Hammer, were jazz-rock fusion, a previously unheard-of style.

Through the 1980s Beck toured and recorded with major stars such as Mick Jagger, Rod Stewart, Tina Turner and Stevie Wonder. He also recorded three albums and won a Grammy. His 2001 release, *You Had It Coming*, earned him another Grammy for Best Rock Instrumental Performance – for the song 'Dirty Mind'.

Jeff Beck has a distinctive style that has influenced many other players. He is a master of melody, whether creating delicate melodies or more aggressive leads. He plays without a plectrum and gets an amazing tonal and dynamic range from his fingers. His bends and vibrato can be aggressive and the whammy bar is an integral part of his style.

GEAR
Guitars: Fender Jeff Beck signature Stratocaster
Amps: Fender Twin Reverbs
Pedals: Vox Tone Bender, Crybaby wah, Colorsound Overdrive, MXR 100 phaser & flanger & 10-band EQ, Maestro Echoplex, Boss OD-1 Overdrive, Boss Chorus Ensemble

ESSENTIAL LISTENING
Cause We've Ended as Lovers (*Blow by Blow*, 1975) • Goodbye Pork Pie Hat (*Wired*, 1976)• Star Cycle (*There and Back*, 1980) • Gets Us All in the End (*Flash*, 1985) • Savoy, Big Block, Where Were You (*Guitar Shop*, 1989) • Space for the Papa, Declan (*Who Else!*, 1999)

ADRIAN BELEW
Although best known for his work with the groundbreaking progressive rock band King Crimson, Adrian Belew has played with some of rock's biggest names over the years: Frank Zappa, David Bowie, Talking Heads, Paul Simon and Nine Inch Nails, to name a few. His solo CDs offer an unlikely melding of pop and avant-garde ideas.

Belew is a versatile player with a distinctly recognizable but quirky style of playing. His rhythm playing is usually augmented by his masterful control over the whammy bar. His solos are often sonically wild, with uncommon sounds and note choices, while his intricate single-note harmony and melody lines are impeccably precise, particularly in his twin guitar tracks with Robert Fripp in King Crimson.

Belew uses an array of off-the-wall sounds, often using (and abusing) effects and equipment to get sounds beyond what the manufacturers intended: over-the-top fuzz; barely controlled chorused feedback; backwards guitar effects; and a lexicon of squeaks, squalls and squeals. He is best known for his ability to simulate the sound of car horns, seagulls, elephants and other natural sounds, and to use them effectively in his music. He has also recorded 'guitar as orchestra' pieces, where the guitar performs the part of every instrument.

GEAR
Guitars: Fender Stratocaster, Parker Fly, Gretsch Chet Atkins
Amps: 2 Johnson Millennium 150, 2 Line6 Vetta II, Line 6 (2x12) extension cabinet
Synths: Roland GR30 guitar synth, Nord Lead III, Korg MS-2000
Pedals: Boss CS-3 compressor, Digitech Whammy II, Sans Amp Comptortion

ESSENTIAL LISTENING
Indiscipline, Discipline, Elephant Talk, Frame By Frame, Thela Hun Ginjeet (King Crimson – *Discipline*, 1981) • Heartbeat (King Crimson – *Beat*, 1982) • Three of a Perfect Pair (King Crimson – *Three of a Perfect Pair*, 1984) • Big Electric Cat, Momur (Adrian Belew – *Lone Rhino*, 1982) • Predatory Feast (Adrian Belew – *Coming Attractions*, 2000) • Writing On The Wall, Matchless Man (Adrian Belew – *Side One*, 2004)

ESSENTIAL VIEWING
King Crimson – Neal and Jack and Me (Live 1982–84) (2004) *King Crimson: Eyes Wide Open* (2003) • *King Crimson: Deja Vroom* (1998)

GEORGE BENSON
It was Wes Montgomery, one of jazz's most creative guitar players, who came across Benson early on; the veteran complimented the young guitarist, urging him to continue his already impressive work. Montgomery had called one of his best records *Boss Guitar*. Benson had both the conviction and chops to nip at his hero's heels; his 1964 debut was released as *The New Boss Guitar*. It certainly lived up to its title. Benson's tone was juicy, and his blues solos sparkled with a carefully honed logic. A jaunty funk-and-swing aesthetic prevailed.

Benson had gained quite a reputation in the industry by the time legendary talent scout John Hammond signed him to Columbia Records. He recorded two successful albums for the label and appeared on a number of other artists' albums, including Miles Davis' *Miles in the Sky*.

Moving to the CTI label in 1970, he worked with many of the finest jazz musicians and became a guitar star. However, wanting to try things like singing along with his guitar he moved to Warner Bros. Records. His first release with Warner was *Breezin'* (1976), the first jazz record ever to attain platinum sales. The track 'This Masquerade', which featured Benson scatting along with his solo break, was a pop smash. He followed up with a sultry version of 'On Broadway', and 'Give Me The Night'. Benson became a superstar.

Benson can play many styles with supreme taste – from swing to bop to R&B and pop. He has a beautiful rounded tone, terrific speed, and a great sense of logic in building solos. Not only can he play lead brilliantly, he is also one of the best rhythm guitarists around, supportive to soloists and a dangerous swinger, particularly in a soul-jazz format.

GEAR
Guitars: Ibanez GB-10 (George Benson)
Amp: Carlos Jazz 'Ash' 60W

ESSENTIAL LISTENING
This Masquerade, Breezin' (George Benson – *Breezin'*, 1976) • Unchained Melody (George Benson – *Livin' Inside Your Love*, 1977) • On Broadway, The Greatest Love of All, Never Give Up on a Good Thing (George Benson – *The George Benson Collection*, 1981)

ESSENTIAL VIEWING
Absolutely Live (George Benson, 2000)

BUCKETHEAD

Buckethead is one of the strangest characters in underground and experimental music. Sporting a Michael Myers mask and an upended Kentucky Fried Chicken bucket on his head, he claims to have been raised by chickens, living in a coop for the first part of his life. This odd dress sense and upbringing has drawn a lot of attention, but there is a phenomenal talent underneath the bucket.

While he is a talented multi-instrumentalist, he is best known for his command of the electric guitar. He is one of the instrument's most recognisable innovators, his idiosyncratic leads and frenetic, hyper-speed riffing, eight-finger solos and angular arpeggios are inspired by rollercoasters and other theme-park rides as well as monster movies. While he shows awesome speed on a fretboard, Buckethead does not just spit out scales; his playing is often laugh-out-loud surprising and always has direction. He has all the technique of Joe Satriani or Steve Vai, but with an extreme psychotic twist and no commercial pretensions whatsoever.

Buckethead's solo career has been productive, and he has recorded and performed with Primus, Guns 'n Roses, Praxis, Iggy Pop, Jonas Hellborg, P-Funk all-stars Bootsy Collins and Bernie Worrell, bassist/producer Bill Laswell and drummer Tony Williams. He has performed on various movie soundtracks, including *The Last Action Hero*, *Mortal Kombat*, *Street Fighter*, *Ghosts of Mars* and *Beverly Hills Ninja*.

GEAR
Guitars: Jackson Flying V, '59 & '69 Gibson Les Paul Custom, Gibson Les Paul Standard Plus
Amps: Marshall JCM-800 & Mesa Boogie Heads
Pedals: Wah Wah
Rack effects: Rocktron Intellifex and Rockman

ESSENTIAL LISTENING
Nun Chuka Kata, Night of the Slunk (*Monsters and Robots*, 1999) • Post Office Buddy, Want Some Slaw?, Welcome to Bucketheadland (*Giant Robot*, 2000)

BUMBLEFOOT (RON THAL)

Ron Thal is a singer, songwriter, composer, producer and engineer. He is well-versed in many styles of music, including classical and jazz. This variety shows in his music, which often has eclectic combinations of sounds and unexpected stylistic shifts. He has a well developed sense of humour, evident in his lyrics, musical arrangements and his playing.

While he is a musical all-rounder, it is on the electric guitar that he really shines. His exuberant guitar pyrotechnics always drive the music forward, rather than the music being a vehicle for the guitar. He uses unorthodox techniques to create sounds that are his own, such as employing a thimble on his right hand to play very high notes or to tap. He is also one of the few guitarists not only to master the fretless guitar, but to advance fretless technique.

Thal was just six years old in 1976 when he heard the *KISS Alive!* album. He knew immediately what he wanted to do. Within two years he was gigging with a band, playing both original music and covers, while continuing his musical studies. At 12 he was conversant with jazz theory, and was a good rhythm player when he heard Van Halen and was inspired to get into soloing. At 13 Ron started putting together a home studio, started recording bands and teaching other kids.

In 1989 Thal recorded a demo, and sent it to *Guitar Player* magazine's Mike Varney for review. Varney was impressed, and Thal signed with Varney's Shrapnel Records in 1994, releasing two CDs before starting his own music production company. Since then he has produced another four albums, accepted being called Bumblefoot (after his first CD) and recorded and produced many more artists.

GEAR
Guitars: Vigier Excalibur, Vigier Bumblefoot Guitar, Vigier Surfreter Fretless
Amps: Line6 Vetta 2X12 Combo
Pedals: Roland GR-30 Guitar Synth, Morley PDW-II Volume/Wah

ESSENTIAL LISTENING
Q Fever (Ron Thal – *The Adventures of Bumblefoot*, 1995) • Hangup, Rowboat (Ron Thal – *Hermit*, 1997) • Noseplugs (Bumblefoot – *Hands*, 1998) • Don Pardo Pimpwagon, Raygun (Bumblefoot – *911*, 2001) • Bagged a Big 1 (Bumblefoot – *Forgotten Anthology*, 2003)

ESSENTIAL VIEWING
Live at the RMA (Bumblefoot, 2004)

ERIC CLAPTON
It is difficult to exaggerate Eric Clapton's impact on blues and rock music, as he has been such an integral part of both since the 1960s. He has made a point of combining these two styles throughout his career – influencing countless guitarists along the way. He is the only triple inductee into the Rock & Roll Hall of Fame.

Clapton played in some of the biggest bands of the rock era: he was still a teen when he joined the Yardbirds in 1963. In 1965 he did one album with John Mayall's Bluesbreakers, then formed Cream in 1966 with Jack Bruce and Ginger Baker, inventing the power trio in hard rock.

Following Cream and the short-lived 'supergroup' Blind Faith, Clapton recorded the classic *Layla & Other Assorted Lovesongs* with Derek and the Dominoes. He then settled into a laid-back period of bluesy solo albums during the early 1970s before returning to mainstream public favour with *Slowhand* (1977). In the 1980s, there were fewer hits but he retained his title as rock's premier bluesman.

Rather than speed or stage show, Eric worked hard on techniques like bends and vibrato. This meant he was always in control of his playing and could be consistent, unlike his contemporaries. He didn't really 'perform' at all – he stood there calmly and played excellent blues-based lead guitar.

Eric was the first guitarist of note to plug a Les Paul into a Marshall amp. (The Vox AC-30 was the standard before him.) However his tone influenced other guitarists to make the switch to Marshalls. He has never used the tremolo bar – even since switching to Fender Strats he has relied on his finger vibrato.

GEAR
Guitars: Fender Stratocaster Clapton Signature, Gibson Les Paul, Gibson SG
Amps: Cornell Eric Clapton Custom 80
Pedals: Roger Mayer Voodoo Vibe, Dunlop GCB-535 CryBaby Multi-Wah

ESSENTIAL LISTENING
Sunshine of Your Love (Cream – *Disraeli Gears*, 1967) • Crossroads, White Room (Cream – *Wheels of Fire*, 1968) • Layla (Derek and the Dominoes – *Layla and Other Assorted Love Songs*, 1970) • Let it Rain (Eric Clapton – *Eric Clapton*, 1970)

ESSENTIAL VIEWING
Eric Clapton and Friends (Eric Clapton, 2003) • *Live in Hyde Park* (Eric Clapton, 2001)

DIMEBAG DARRELL
While most hard rock guitarists of the early 1990s were focusing on songwriting rather than technical ability, 'Dimebag' Darrell Abbott was playing punishing riffs and shredding solos. He stuck to doing what he felt was right, rather than changing his style to fit in with musical trends. His 'scooped' (midrange cut) rhythm tone became the standard for metal guitarists. He was one of the first players to popularize the DigiTech Whammy pedal, which influenced bands such as Korn and Rage Against the Machine.

Dimebag was born into a musical family and it wasn't long before he discovered the band KISS and became interested in rock guitar. Together with his drummer brother

Vinnie Paul, Dimebag formed Pantera in the early 1980s, and developed his signature style. While Pantera reflected the influence of Def Leppard and Mötley Crüe, their sound later became much more brutal, owing more to Slayer and Metallica. A string of classic metal releases such as *Cowboys From Hell*, *Vulgar Display of Power*, and *Far Beyond Driven* saw Pantera become one of the world's top metal bands.

Dimebag and Vinnie Paul formed a new metal band called Damageplan in the early 21st century. He also appeared on recordings by other artists, including Anthrax and Nickelback.

In December 2004 Dimebag was shot and killed by a concertgoer while on stage with Damageplan. His untimely death sent shockwaves throughout the music community where he is remembered as one of the most influential stylists in modern metal.

GEAR
Guitars: Washburn 333 Dimebag Darrell, Washburn Stealth Dimebag, Washburn Culprit Dimebag
Amps: Six Randall Warhead 300Watt Heads driving six 4X12 Warhead Cabs and two 1X15 cabs
Pedals: Digitech WH-1 Whammy Original, Dunlop 535Q Wah Pedal, Whirlwind A/B Selector
Rack Effects: Furman PQ-3B Parametric EQ, Korg DTR-1 Tuner, Rocktron Guitar Silencer

ESSENTIAL LISTENING
Domination, Cemetary gates (Pantera – *Cowboys From Hell*, 1990) • Hollow (Pantera – *Vulgar Display of Power*, 1992) • Floods, The Great Southern Trendkill (Pantera – *The Great Southern Trendkill*, 1998)

ESSENTIAL VIEWING
3 – Vulgar Videos from Hell (Pantera, 1999)

AL DI MEOLA
Al Di Meola is best known for his astounding speed, and has often been criticized for playing with less feeling than velocity. However, over the course of a long career, he has proved that he can do both equally well. He also has the ability to maintain a sense of melody, regardless of speed or style – a trait many of his peers do not always show.

His prolific career has bridged a wide range of styles, from rapid, machine-gun-like scales with provocative, lyrical melodies to the fiery passion of Latin-influenced melodies.

Di Meola studied at Berklee College of Music in Boston, where he was known for his marathon practice sessions. In 1974, at the age of 19, he joined Chick Corea's Return To

Forever, a top fusion band, and made his name as an almost impossibly fleet-fingered soloist.

Di Meola began recording under his own name two years later, immediately building on his reputation as formidable fusion guitarist with the albums *Land of the Midnight Sun* and *Elegant Gypsy*. Since then he has released dozens of albums, using a number of different approaches on both classical and electric instruments. He has also recorded on acoustic guitar, mandolin and guitar synthesizer.

Over the years he has recorded or played with a host of major artists, including Chick Corea, Luciano Pavarotti, Paco De Lucia, Paul Simon, Phil Collins, Santana, John McLaughlin, Larry Coryell, Steve Winwood, Wayne Shorter, Herbie Hancock, Jaco Pastorius, Les Paul, Jean-Luc Ponty, Steve Vai, Frank Zappa, Egberto Gismonti, Jimmy Page, Milton Nascimento, Tony Williams, Stanley Clarke, Stevie Wonder, Irakere and many more.

GEAR
Guitars: PRS Guitars
Amps: Koch Multitone 100w combo amplifiers

ESSENTIAL LISTENING
The Magician (Return to Forever – *Romantic Warrior*, 1976) • Golden Dawn Suite (Al Di Meola – *Land of the Midnight Sun*, 1976) • Race With The Devil On Spanish Highway (Al Di Meola – *Elegant Gypsy*, 1977) • Nena (Al Di Meola – *Tour De Force*, 1982) • Cruisin' (Al Di Meola – *Electric Rendezvous*, 1982)

ESSENTIAL VIEWING
One of These Nights (Al Di Meola, 2005) • *Live at Montreux* (Al Di Meola, 2004) • *Al Di Meola* (Al Di Meola, 1992)

JERRY DONAHUE
'Bend Master of the Telecaster' is the moniker bestowed upon Jerry Donahue by those fortunate enough to have witnessed first-hand his amazing, almost freakish electric guitar technique, both as a soloist and as one third of The Hellecasters.

Donahue began playing piano at the age of six, just after the family's move from New York to Hollywood. Shifting his focus to the guitar at age 12, his passion for the instrument became evident as he absorbed the musical influences of the day, from Duane Eddy to Chuck Berry to The Ventures to Chet Atkins to The Shadows. Moving to England at age 14, Jerry combined the folk music of his adopted home with his American rock, blues and country roots to produce his unmistakable style.

Jerry has received widespread acclaim for his work as a member of The Hellecasters guitar trio. In 1994, *Guitar Shop*

magazine described Jerry as a 'freak of nature' whose string-bending technique could be accomplished only by a 'four-armed pedal steeler!' The late, great Danny Gatton referred to him as 'the string-bending king of the planet'. Jerry has also won many *Guitar Player* magazine Reader's Poll awards.

Jerry Donahue has performed and recorded with some of the biggest names in popular music. From his early days in such folk-influenced bands as Fotheringay and Fairport Convention; through his recordings with Gerry Rafferty, Joan Armatrading, Chris Rea, The Proclaimers, John Illsley (Dire Straits), Johnny Hallyday, and Nancy Griffith. He has also recorded with Robert Plant, Elton John, Gary Wright, George Harrison, Cliff Richard, Bruce Welch, Hank Marvin, Warren Zevon, Bonnie Raitt, and Roy Orbison, and is renowned as the consummate 'guitarist's guitarist'.

GEAR
Guitars: Fender Jerry Donahue Telecaster, Fender Jerry Donahue Stratocaster.
Amps: Sessionmaster JD-10 preamp into a Fender Hot Rod Deville amp
Pedals: Nobels ODR 1 overdrive

ESSENTIAL LISTENING
Orange Blossom Special, Menage: The Beak/The Claw (The Hellcasters – *Return Of The Hellecasters*, 1993) • Axe To Grind (The Hellcasters – *Escape From Hollywood*, 1994) • T.W.P.P.T, Mad Cows At Ease, Breaking Through (The Hellcasters – *Hell III – New Axes To Grind*, 1997)

MIKE EINZIGER
Mike Einziger, guitarist for Incubus, is an original, an eclectic and often surprising player who combines funk, metal and jazz elements. He uses interesting and unusual combinations of sounds and styles to create a tapestry of textured sonic assault. His tonal palette consists of everything from raw walls of distortion through crunchy rhythms to delicate spacious atmospheres. Most importantly, Einziger knows how and when to use his varied sounds, stylings and not inconsiderable technique – he does what the music requires without overplaying.

Born in Los Angeles, in 1976, Einziger was turned on to Van Halen at age six. However as he had very small hands he did not take up the guitar immediately, taking up drums, flute and piano instead. Then at age 12, his interest in Van Halen was rekindled after hearing a friend's brother playing 'Eruption'.

Incubus was formed in in 1991 by Einziger and school friends Brandon Boyd, Alex Katunich and José Pasillas. The quartet began playing at shows and parties before moving on to the bars and clubs of Los Angeles. During this period the band recruited DJ Lyfe, who added a hip-hop element to their eclectic mix of funk, metal and jazz. This sound, combined with their electrifying live shows and assiduous self-promotion, generated a buzz, and after the independent release of their first CD, *Fungus Amongus*, they signed to Immortal Records in 1995.

Since then, Incubus have released a number of albums, including 1999's double-platinum *Make Yourself*, and 2001's *Morning View*, which debuted at No. 2 on the *Billboard* 200.

GEAR
Guitars: PRS Archtop, PRS Hollowbody, PRS Custom 24
Amps: Mesa Boogie Dual Rectifier Tremoverb with two Mesa Boogie 4 X 12 cabinets
Pedals: Hughs & Kettner Rotosphere, Boss Digital Delay, Boss PH-2 Phaser, DOD FX13, Digitech Genesis III, Digitech Whammy 4
Rack: Korg Rack Tuner

ESSENTIAL LISTENING
Pardon Me, Stellar, Privilege (Incubus – *Make Yourself*, 1999) • Sick Sad Little World, Priceless (Incubus – *A Crow Left of the Murder*, 2004)

ESSENTIAL VIEWING
When Incubus Attacks: Vol. 1 (Incubus, 2000) • *When Incubus Attacks Vol. 2* (Incubus, 2001) • *Morning View* (Incubus, 2001)

MATTIAS 'IA' EKLUNDH
Swedish guitarist Mattias 'IA' Eklundh started out as a drummer at the age of six after buying a Kiss record. After seeing a Frank Zappa concert when he was 11 he was inspired to dive head first into playing the guitar. Self-taught, he borrowed books from the library to learn music theory.

After playing in the groups Frozen Eyes and Fate during the late 1980s, Eklundh formed Freak Kitchen in 1992, with whom he has recorded five CDs to date. In 1999 he released his first solo CD, *Freak Guitar*, a monumental, six-string roller-coaster ride. The follow-up, the astonishing *The Road Less Travelled*, was released in 2004.

Eklundh is unique in the instrumental guitar genre. His music spans a wide spectrum of styles, from Frank Zappa insanity, through gypsy jazz and samba to screaming hard rock excess. His playing incorporates amazing shredding, clever tapping and deft whammy bar use, all combined with unusual melodies, polyrhythms, odd time and unorthodox techniques that keep it fresh and interesting.

Despite the huge array of often unusual sounds he creates, he uses no equipment beyond guitar, wah pedal and amplifier. He is often asked what brand of whammy pedal he owns, which amuses him.

Every year he takes three groups of advanced guitarists into the Swedish wilderness for the Freak Guitar Camp. This is a week of workshops covering everything from theory, unusual techniques and the music business. The pace is intense as 10 hours a day are spent just on lessons, with any other waking hours spent practising.

GEAR
Guitars: Caparison Apple Horn 27 fret electric
Amps: Laney VH100R and straight GS cabinets
Pedals: Wah Pedal

ESSENTIAL LISTENING
La Bamba (Mattias Eklundh – *Freak Guitar*, 1999) • Gun God, Sinking Planet (Freak Kitchen – *Dead Soul Men*, 2000) • Nobody's Laughing Here (Freak Kitchen – *Move*, 2002) • The Road Less Travelled, There's No Money in Jazz, Print This! (Mattias Eklundh – *The Road Less Travelled*, 2004)

ESSENTIAL VIEWING
Freak Guitar Vol. 1 (Mattias Eklundh, 1994) • *United* (Various Artists, 2005)

ROBERT FRIPP
Robert Fripp has been a fixture on the contemporary music scene since 1969. Throughout his career, he has continually pushed the boundaries of pop music, as well as pursuing avant-garde and experimental musical ideas.

Fripp began playing professionally in the mid-1960s, providing instrumental support to many American singers who were touring the UK. During this time he formed a trio that evolved into one of the most respected progressive rock bands of the era – King Crimson. From 1969 to date, Fripp has been the mainstay of King Crimson, leading it through its various musical incarnations.

The harmonic invention and sheer technical virtuosity of early King Crimson were unprecedented in rock. Robert Fripp's tone was at times delicate and nuanced, at others devastatingly distorted, and his Les Paul could sing with electrifying and seemingly infinite sustain.

Fripp is a very knowledgeable musician, having started to devise his own guitar method at age 12. He has also developed his own tuning system, which he has used since 1975.

Fripp's work is highly original, often with extreme distortion, unusual modalities, complex meters, polymeter, precisely controlled instrumental textures and ambiguous tonality. He has also developed 'Frippertronics', which involves long delays with sustained fuzz tones. Some of the later King Crimson music is characterized by two over-lapping guitar lines played in different times so as to sound like unusual delay effects. He will often use harmonizers or guitar synths to create surreal, shifting soundscapes with haunting atmospheres.

GEAR
Guitars: Fernandes Electric Guitar w/ Sustainer
Pedals: Digitech WH-1 Whammy, Rocktron Midi Foot Controller, Roland GR-1 Guitar Synth, Roland GR-30 Guitar Synth, Roland VG-8,
Rack Gear: Eventide H3000/3500 Harmonizer, Roland GP-100 Preamp/FX, TC Electronic 2290 Digital Delay, TC Electronic G-Force Multi-FX

ESSENTIAL LISTENING
21st Century Schizoid Man (King Crimson – *In the Court of the Crimson King*, 1969) • Discipline, Frame By Frame (King Crimson – *Discipline*, 1981) • Three of a Perfect Pair, Larks Tongues in Aspic Part III (King Crimson – *Three of a Perfect Pair*, 1984) • God Save the King (League of Gentlemen – *God Save the King*, 1985)

ESSENTIAL VIEWING
King Crimson – Neal and Jack and Me (2004) • *King Crimson: Eyes Wide Open* (2003) • *King Crimson: Deja Vroom* (1998)

DAVID GILMOUR
Over the course of Pink Floyd's career David Gilmour has developed and retained a unique and recognizable voice. He is known for his distinctively spacey, atmospheric guitar work, soaring, melodic solos and impressive use of vibrato.

Gilmour is highly regarded by many guitarists by sheer virtue of his expressive playing, often being mentioned in the same breath as Clapton, Page or Beck. While he does not have the technical ability of many younger guitarists, he has a clearly defined sound and style that are his own.

Gilmour's ability and desire to experiment with sounds have led him to amass a frightening array of effects, including many rare and vintage models as well as a number of one-off prototypes which never made it to production.

While known for his extensive, complex and often subtle effects usage, Gilmour's signature sound comes more from his playing than from his effects. Renowned producer Bob Ezrin has said of him: 'With Gilmour, equipment is secondary to touch. You can give him a ukulele and he'll make it sound like a Stradivarius.'

GEAR
Guitars: Fender Stratocasters & Telecasters
Amps: 6 Hiwatt AP-100 100W heads powering: Two Marshall 4 x 12" cabs, Two WEM 4 x 12" cabs, 3 Doppola custom rotating speakers
Pedals: three Cry-Baby Sweep Pedals, volume pedal, wah-wah, Electro-Harmonix Electric Mistress Flanger, Electro-Harmonix Big Muff fuzz, MXR Phase 90, Orange Treble and Bass Booster, Arbiter Fuzz Face, Noise Gate, MXR Digital Delay, Boss CS-2 Compressor Pro Co. Rat II Distortion, Cornish Big Muff, Three Boss GE-7 Graphic EQs, Cornish Soft Sustain, Sovtek Big Muff II, Two Chandler Tube Driver, MXR Dynacomp Compressor, Ibanez CP-9 Compressor, Boss Metalizer, Boss HM-2 Heavy Metal Distortion.
Rack gear: T.C. Electronics 2290 Digital Delay, Binson Echorec tape echo, Uni-Vibe, Digitech IPS-33B Super Harmony Machine, Lexicon PCM-70 Digital Effects Processor, Dynachord CL5222 Leslie Simulator

ESSENTIAL LISTENING
Time (Pink Floyd – *Dark Side of The Moon*, 1973) • Shine on you Crazy Diamond Parts 1-5 (Pink Floyd – *Wish You Were Here*, 1975) • Dogs (Pink Floyd – *Animals*, 1977) • Another Brick in the Wall Part 2, Comfortably Numb (Pink Floyd – *The Wall*, 1979)

ESSENTIAL VIEWING
Pink Floyd PULSE Live in Earls Court London (1995) • *David Gilmour in Concert* (2002) • *Pink Floyd – Live at Pompeii* (2003)

JIMI HENDRIX
Jimi Hendrix permanently changed the course of rock music. He expanded the vocabulary of the electric guitar and influenced more players than anyone else. Hendrix was a master at coaxing all manner of sounds from his instrument, and was a consummate showman; he would play behind his back, with his teeth and even set his guitar alight.

Hendrix grew up listening to the blues, taking up guitar in his teens. He played in various R&B bands before moving to England and forming The Jimi Hendrix Experience. Success came quickly, with three singles making the Top Ten in the first half of 1967. Their debut album, *Are You Experienced?*, stunned the guitar world. His next three albums further astounded and inspired, and his performance at Woodstock made history. Sadly, he was dead of a drug overdose by 1970 – just short of 28 years of age.

Hendrix's style was based on the blues, with influences from R&B, rock, funk, jazz and country music. His rapier-like runs vied with measured solos, matching energy with ingenuity. His rhythm work featured a relaxed picking style that let him play very funky rhythms, and he would often throw in short fills and phrases.

Hendrix was left-handed and played his guitars upside-down, just reversing the strings, and he tuned down to Eb to make bending easier. While he is often associated with distortion, Jimi also had beautiful clean tones. His recorded tone was very clean by today's standards, and his effect usage brought texture to his overall sound.

GEAR
Guitars: Fender Stratocaster
Amps: Marshall 100Watt Plexi Heads and Marshall 4x12 Cabinets
Pedals: Dallas Arbiter Fuzz Face, Roger Mayer Octavia Fuzz/Octave, UniVox UniVibe, Vox Wah

ESSENTIAL LISTENING
Purple Haze, Fire (The Jimi Hendrix Experience – *Are You Experienced?*, 1967) • Little Wing (The Jimi Hendrix Experience – *Axis: Bold as Love*, 1967) • All Along The Watchtower, Voodoo Chile (Slight Return) (The Jimi Hendrix Experience – *Electric Ladyland*, 1968) • Machine Gun (Band of Gypsies – *Band of Gypsies*, 1970)

ESSENTIAL VIEWING
Blue Wild Angel (Live at the Isle of Wight) 2002 • *Jimi Hendrix – Live at Woodstock* (1999)

ALLAN HOLDSWORTH
One of a handful of musicians who has been an innovator in both rock and jazz music, Allan Holdsworth is often regarded as one of the finest guitarists of the 20th century. He has been cited by many instrumental masters (including Steve Vai, Frank Zappa and Joe Satriani) as a unique and inspirational player.

In the 1970s Holdsworth gained attention playing with progressive groups such as Soft Machine, Bruford, U.K., Gong and Jean-Luc Ponty. He later launched a solo career, which has seen the release of more than 16 albums. While these works have mostly not seen large scale commercial success, albums such as *Metal Fatigue*, *Atavachron* and *Sand and Secrets* stand out as both innovative and creative.

Holdsworth has often worked with, and helped develop, guitar technology in a ceaseless quest to expand his tonal palette. During the late 1980s, the Synthaxe (a guitar-based synthesizer controller) was the key to Holdsworth's entirely unique sound. This guitar synthesizer enabled him to explore an untold number of textures and colours lacking in the conventional six-string vocabulary. He has

designed baritone electric guitars, most recently manufactured by Carvin. He has also invented electronic components for the recording studio.

Holdsworth's style consists of unconventional, expansive chord voicings – often with tightly clustered intervals – which create shifting melodies and harmonies. His solos contain fluid legato lines and passionate melodic phrases. He has a masterful ability to improvize over complex chord voicings. He has one of the most identifiable guitar voices in modern music, with horn-like phrasing and tone.

GEAR
Guitars: Bill DeLap headless guitar, Allan Holdsworth Carvin Fatboy
Amps: Yamaha DG80 112 digital modelling amps loaded with Celestion Vintage 30s
Pedals: Two Yamaha UD Stomps

ESSENTIAL LISTENING
Devil Take the Hindmost, Metal Fatigue (Allan Holdsworth – *Metal Fatigue*, 1985) • Lanyard Loop, The Things You See (Allan Holdsworth – *All Night Wrong*, 2002) • San Onofre, The Sixteen Men of Tain (Allan Holdsworth – *The Sixteen Men of Tain*, 2000)

ESSENTIAL VIEWING
Allan Holdsworth (Allan Holdsworth, 2000) • *Live at the Galaxy Theatre* (Allan Holdsworth, 2002)

STANLEY JORDAN
Jazz guitarist Stanley Jordan's pianistic approach to two-handed tapping is unique. While players like Eddie Van Halen embellish their solos with fast two-handed technique, Jordan plays compositions and solos that feature fully independent chords, bass lines and melodies.

Jordan was born in Chicago in 1959. He started playing piano at age six, and changed to guitar at 11. He retained his keyboard technique, however, which provided the basis for the touch system of playing, which he developed in his mid-teens. Finding standard guitar tuning illogical, he also began to tune his instrument in fourths (E, A, D, G, C, F, low to high), which is the tuning he still uses.

Jordan studied at Princeton University, earning a degree in music theory and composition, but he chose to make a living as a street musician, playing in New York, Philadelphia and various towns in the Midwest and South. Before long, word spread about an incredible guitarist playing for pocket change on the street. He was soon offered a contract with the revived Blue Note Records and became the label's first new artist.

In 1985 Jordan released *Magic Touch*, which was produced by Al Di Meola. The album quickly rocketed to the top of *Billboard*'s jazz charts, staying there for 49 weeks. It also made a surprising jump to the pop charts.

Much of the attention surrounding his sudden rise to fame was based on his playing technique – it is so unusual that it makes a dominating first impression. However, through the years it become clear that Jordan has musicianship and creativity to match his technique. Since the early 1980s he has focused much more on expressiveness than on speed and complexity.

GEAR
Guitars: Ibanez Roadstar, Travis Bean
Amps: Roland JC-120

ESSENTIAL LISTENING
Elanor Rigby, The Lady in My Life, All the Children, Freddie Freeloader (*Magic Touch*, 1985) • Georgia On My Mind (*Standards Volume 1*, 1986) • Impressions (*Cornucopia*, 1990)

MARK KNOPFLER
Mark Knopfler is a guitarist, singer, songwriter and bandleader whose distinctive guitar style has had a substantial impact on the guitar community, affecting otherwise identifiable stylists such as Eric Clapton and Carlos Santana.

Knopfler's group, Dire Straits, formed in 1977, became an international success in the wake of the release of its self-titled debut album in 1978. Though Dire Straits started out as a group, it evolved into a kind of brand for Knopfler, with varying personnel.

Knopfler has forged his own distinctive sound by combining some of the best aspects of traditional and contemporary musical styles. As with many other great British guitarists, Knopfler became enchanted with the blues at a very early age. He also explored folk, skiffle, ragtime, country blues, jugband, and even western swing styles.

Playing with his fingers, Knopfler's plectrum-less guitar style is as varied as it is distinctive, with eccentric melodicism, extensive use of hammer-ons and pull-offs, tasteful vibrato and laid-back melodies.

While he is best known for his 'out-of-phase' Stratocaster tone (bridge and middle pickups combined), his later work also features a throaty, almost cello-like Les Paul lead sound.

Knopfler has also recorded with Chet Atkins, the Notting Hillbillies, James Taylor, Van Morrison, and Squeeze leaders Glenn Tilbrook and Chris Difford, Steely Dan, Van Morrison, Thin Lizzy's Phil Lynott, Phil Everly, as well as with Bob Dylan and The Shadows.

GEAR
Guitars: Fender Mark Knopfler Signature Strat, Gibson Les Paul, Pensa Suhr, Schecter Strat
Amps: Crate Vintage Club VC5212, Soldano SLO 100 with Hughes & Kettner 2 x 12 cabinets
Pedals: Ernie Ball volume pedal, Active Lead, TC2290 delay unit, Lexicon 300 reverb unit, MXR micro amp and a TC 0144 footswitch.

ESSENTIAL LISTENING
Sultans of Swing (Dire Straits – *Dire Straits*, 1978) • Brothers in Arms (Dire Straits – *Brothers in Arms*, 1985) • Telegraph Road (Dire Straits – *Love Over Gold*, 1982) • Yakety Axe (Chet Atkins & Mark Knopfler – *Neck and Neck*, 1990) • Fade to Black (Dire Straits – *On Every Street*, 1991) • Boom Like That (Mark Knopfler – *Sailing To Philadelphia*, 2004)

ESSENTIAL VIEWING
On the Night (Dire Straits, 2004) • *A Night in London* (Mark Knopfler, 2004) • *Sultans of Swing: the Very Best of...* (Dire Straits, 2000)

SHAWN LANE
Shawn Lane was a phenomenally talented guitar player whose fame never spread beyond guitar enthusiasts, but will remain influential to players for many years to come.

A child prodigy, Lane began his musical education on piano and cello at age four, but had switched to guitar by age eight. At ten, he was holding band rehearsals in his home, and since the other band members left their instruments at his house, Lane learned to play them too.

He began his professional career at the age of 15, joining the Southern rock band Black Oak Arkansas in 1978. He never released an album with them, but videos showed he was already an impressive player. He then dropped out of sight in 1982 to concentrate on his piano playing and to study music theory and composition.

Lane next appeared in cover bands playing in clubs, and he formed a band called the Willys who were the house band at the Peabody Hotel in Memphis. Many touring musicians caught Lane's playing while staying there, and word of mouth led to session work. On the strength of this work he earned a recording contract.

In 1992 Lane released his first solo album *Powers Of Ten*. He played all the instruments, composed, engineered and produced everything himself. Following its release, *Guitar Player* magazine named him 'Best New Talent' and *Keyboard* magazine placed him second in the 'Best Keyboard Player' category. Even with all the acclaim, he somehow remained an underground guitar hero.

In 1994 Lane teamed up with Swedish bassist Jonas Hellborg, with whom he had a common interest in world music and fusion and they released eight CDs together. He also released his second solo work, *The Tritone Fascination* and *Powers Of Ten Live*.

After developing health problems in 2001, he passed away on 26 September 2003, following surgery.

GEAR
Guitars: Vigier Excalibur Supra, Vigier Excalibur Surfreter fretless
Amps: Peavey TransTube FEX preamp
Pedals: Line6 DL4 Delay Modeller

ESSENTIAL LISTENING
Get You Back, Gray Pianos Flying (Shawn Lane – *Powers of Ten*, 1992) • The Way It Has To Be (Shawn Lane – *The Tri-Tone Fascination*, 2000) • Hardcase (Shawn Lane – *Powers Of Ten Live*, 2001)

TONY MACALPINE

Tony MacAlpine is a classic overachiever. He is not only one of the best virtuoso guitar shredders to emerge after the Yngwie Malmsteen invasion, but is also an excellent classical pianist. This progressive metal guitar virtuoso began his musical education as a classically trained pianist and violinist; his subsequent rock recordings retained a pronounced classical influence, incorporating elements of jazz and fusion as well.

MacAlpine debuted in 1986 with the instrumental *Edge of Insanity*, recorded with an all-star line-up including bassist Billy Sheehan and ex-Journey drummer Steve Smith. For the follow-up, *Project: Driver*, MacAlpine formed the band M.A.R.S. with drummer Tommy Aldridge, vocalist Bob Rock and bassist Rudi Sarzo. The group soon dissolved and MacAlpine returned to his solo career, additionally forming his own label, Squawk.

After 1987's *Maximum Security*, he founded another group, dubbed MacAlpine, with singer Alan Schorn, keyboardist Mark Robertson, bassist Mike Jacques and drummer Billy Carmassi. The band's lone record, *Eyes of the World*, appeared in 1990, and MacAlpine returned to instrumental projects for the rest of the decade, issuing a series of albums including 1992's *Freedom to Fly*, 1995's *Evolution*, 1997's and 2000's *CAB. CAB 2* followed in 2001. *CAB 4* was released on Favored Nations Records in 2004.

In 2001 MacAlpine started touring with guitar maestro Steve Vai, as second guitarist and keyboardist. This band also saw him reunited with master bassist Billy Sheehan. This landmark tour was memorably captured on the *Steve Vai: Live at the Astoria London* DVD. Trading riffs with Vai, MacAlpine shows just how talented and accomplished he is.

GEAR
Guitars: Carvin TMAC VI, Carvin TMAC VII
Amps: Carvin Legacy Head, Marshall 4 x 12 cabinet

ESSENTIAL LISTENING
Autumn Lords, Hundreds of Thousands (*Maximum Security*, 1986) • The Violin Song (*Premonition*, 1994) • Cab, Bernard (Cab – *MacAlpine/Brunel/Chambers*, 2000)

ESSENTIAL VIEWING
Live at the Astoria London (Steve Vai, 2004) • *G3 Live in Denver* (G3, 2004)

YNGWIE MALMSTEEN

Yngwie Malmsteen was one of the most technically accomplished hard rock guitarists to emerge during the 1980s. His playing was astonishingly fast and fiery, with a strong Baroque flavour and gothic compositional style. The pyrotechnics on his mostly instrumental debut album, *Rising Force*, had a major influence on the 'shredding' guitarists, with their focus on fast playing.

Malmsteen first took up the guitar at age seven, on the day Jimi Hendrix died, after seeing clips of Hendrix's playing on a television special. He soon became obsessed with the guitar, practising up to nine hours a day, learning the music of his influences – Hendrix and Deep Purple's Ritchie Blackmore. The classical flavour of Blackmore's playing led him to explore the work of classical composers like Bach and Beethoven.

At age 10, Malmsteen discovered Niccolò Paganini, the 19th-century Italian composer and violinist who was legendary for his amazing ability on his instrument. Paganini's challenging *24 Caprices* provided a blueprint for Malmsteen's synthesis of classical music and rock. Moreover, Paganini's flamboyant style and larger-than-life ego also provided Malmsteen with a template for dealing with the music press and his critics.

Malmsteen is not as popular as he once was, thanks partly to a backlash against the shredding that he is linked with, and the fact that his music has progressed very little since he first appeared. However, when taken in small doses, his music is still staggering in its technical facility.

Malmsteen's ultra-fast scales and arpeggios are possible partly due to the deeply scalloped fingerboards he uses. He plays with masses of amplifiers and very high gain, so he fits his guitars with DiMarzio stacked humbuckers to avoid feedback and hum.

GEAR
Guitars: Fender Yngwie Malmsteen Stratocaster
Amps: 28 Marshall JMP-50 MKII Heads with 31 Marshall 4 X 12 Cabinets
Pedals: Dunlop Cry Baby Wah, Vox Flanger
Rack Effects: Two Korg DL-8000R Delays, T.C. Electronic G-Force Multi-Effects, Korg SDD-2000 Digital Delay, Rocktron Hush IICX Noise Gate

ESSENTIAL LISTENING
Black Star, Icarus' Dream Suite (Yngwie Malmsteen – *Rising Force*, 1984) • Marching Out (Yngwie Malmsteen – *Marching Out*, 1985) • Trilogy Suite Op-5 (Yngwie Malmsteen – *Trilogy*, 1986) • Blitzkrieg (Yngwie Malmsteen – *Alchemy*, 1999) • Baroque and Roll (Yngwie Malmsteen – *Attack*, 2002)

ESSENTIAL VIEWING
Live in Denver (G3, 2003) • *Live!* (Yngwie Malmsteen, 2000)

BRIAN MAY
Queen guitarist and songwriter Brian May has long been the king of multi-tracked guitar harmonies and well-constructed melodic leads. He has a playing style that is instantly recognizable anywhere.

May showed musical aptitude at a young age: he could already play the ukulele and piano by the time he was given his first guitar, on his seventh birthday. The young May was influenced by early rock and roll guitarists such as Buddy Holly, Scotty Moore and Hank Marvin, and joined a band called 1984 during his school days. The band enjoyed some success, opening for major acts such as Jimi Hendrix, Pink Floyd, Traffic and T-Rex. May left 1984 to study physics and mathematics at college. During his studies he met Roger Taylor and formed the band Smile.

After graduating, May focused on music, and Smile was renamed Queen after Freddie Mercury joined as vocalist. By 1973 the band had signed a record deal and released their first album. The 1975 album, *A Night at the Opera*, became a huge hit, yielding the classic single, 'Bohemian Rhapsody'. Subsequent releases saw them gain in popularity. By the late 1970s, Queen were one of the world's most popular bands.

May and his father built his unique 'Red Special' guitar from scratch from inexpensive materials (such as an old mahogany fireplace). The 'Red Special' remains May's main guitar to this day. A few companies such as Burns and RS Guitars now make Red Special replicas.

May has been a great influence on other renowned rock guitarists past and present, including Billy Corgan (Smashing Pumpkins) and Nuno Bettencourt (Population 1).

GEAR
Guitars: Homemade 'Red Special'
Amps: Four Vox AC-30TB
Pedals: Glen Fryer Custom Treble Booster, Dunlop Cry-Baby Wah, Rocktron Midi Mate Foot Controller.
Rack effects: Rocktron Intellifex, Two Bel delays, Rocktron Patch Mate switcher.

ESSENTIAL LISTENING
Killer Queen (Queen – *Sheer Heart Attack*, 1974) • Bohemian Rhapsody, Love of My Life (Queen – *A Night at the Opera*, 1975) • We Are the Champions, We Will Rock You (Queen – *News of the World*, 1977) • Fat Bottomed Girls, Don't Stop Me Now (Queen – *Jazz*, 1978)

ESSENTIAL VIEWING
Greatest Video Hits 1 (Queen, 2002) • *Live at Wembley Stadium* (Queen, 2003) • *On Fire at the Bowl* (Queen, 2004)

JOHN MCLAUGHLIN
John McLaughlin is an innovative guitarist who stands out as one of the most intense virtuosos ever. His aim was to achieve a level of guitar playing comparable to that of Miles Davis, John Coltrane and Ornette Coleman on their instruments. He thrives on developing new musical forms and has pioneered fusions of jazz, Eastern, classical and rock music.

McLaughlin studied piano from the age of nine. He took up the guitar when he was 11, and by the time he was 14 had become interested in flamenco and jazz.

McLaughlin was one of the architects of fusion. Jazz guitarists before him used predictable, quiet sounds, but McLaughlin's volume changed that. In addition to founding and leading the Mahavishnu Orchestra, Shakti and the John McLaughlin Trio, he has worked with Miles Davis, Carlos Santana, Billy Cobham, Michael Tilson Thomas, Chick Corea, David Sanborn, Trilok Gurtu, Elvin Jones and many more.

McLaughlin's playing incorporates long melody lines, odd time signatures, blisteringly fast, ever-ascending runs, elusive harmonies and razor-sharp rhythmic patterns. All of these elements were new when he introduced them back in 1970. Even now his recordings sound fresh and exciting.

Never one to shy away from technology, McLaughlin was an early convert to guitar synthesizers, and currently uses a computer as an amp and synthesizers.

GEAR
Guitars: '68 Gibson Johnny Smith
Rack Gear: Roland GI-10 Guitar to MIDI interface, Sony DPS-V77 or DPS-M7signal processor
Computer: Apple Powerbook notebook with MOTU 828

Software: Logic and Logic plug-ins, Mac and Logic soft-synths.

ESSENTIAL LISTENING

A Love Supreme (John McLaughlin & Carlos Santana – *Love Devotion Surrender*, 1973) • Sister Andrea (Mahavishnu Orchestra – *Between Nothingness & Eternity*, 1973) • Vision is a Naked Sword (Mahavishnu Orchestra – *Apocalypse*, 1974) • New York On My Mind, Friendship (John McLaughlin – *Electric Guitarist*, 1978) • The Dark Prince, The Unknown Dissident (John Mclaughlin & The One Truth Band – *Electric Dreams*, 1979)

ESSENTIAL VIEWING

Best Of Jazz Open 1998 (2001) • *Meeting of the Spirits* (1981) • *This Is The Way I Do It* (2004)

TOM MORELLO

With Rage Against the Machine (RATM) and Audioslave, Tom Morello's unusual playing style has made him one of the most exciting players to surface in years. He incorporates a myriad styles and sounds into his playing, coaxing unheard-of sounds from his home-made Frankenstein guitar. 'No samples, keyboards or synthesizers used in the making of this recording', claims the RATM liner notes. And with Morello's every fill and solo being so unusual, this claim is necessary.

As a teenager, the mostly self-taught Morello was infatuated with rock music and practised up to eight hours a day. His influences were players like Hendrix and Page, who continually sought new ways to broaden their sonic palettte.

His first band achieved no impact before its demise, so Morello planned that his next venture would be more politically minded, with a harder musical edge. Rage Against the Machine was formed in 1991, and over the course of a four-album career became one of rock's leading bands.

When RATM's vocalist left, Morello and the rest of the band enlisted former Soundgarden singer Chris Cornell, forming a group that would be renamed Audioslave.

While he often uses a whammy pedal, Morello's unorthodox techniques for making odd sounds with his guitar often rely more on mechanical methods – like faulty pickup selector switches and scraping strings with allen keys – than effects processors.

GEAR

Guitars: Home-made Strat-Style Electric, Fender Telecaster Standard Electric, Goya Rangemaster, Ibanez Custom Semi-Hollow Body
Amps: Marshall JCM-800 Head Peavey Cabinet/4 x 12
Pedals: Boss DD-2 Digital Delay, Digitech WH-1 Whammy, DOD FX-40B Equalizer, Dunlop CryBaby Wah Pedal, Ibanez DFL Flanger

ESSENTIAL LISTENING

Killing In The Name, Bullet in the Head (Rage Against The Machine – *Rage Against The Machine*, 1992) • Calm Like a Bomb, Voice of the Voiceless (Rage Against The Machine – *The Battle of Los Angeles*, 1999) • Cochise, Like A Stone (Audioslave – *Audioslave*, 2002)

ESSENTIAL VIEWING

Rage Against the Machine: The Battle of Mexico City (2000) • *Rage Against The Machine – Live at the Grand Olympic Auditorium* (2003)

JIMMY PAGE

Jimmy Page is best known for his classic work with Led Zeppelin and the Yardbirds. His live performances and recordings with Led Zeppelin influenced most rock guitarists from the 1970s to today. His riffs served as the blueprint for what would eventually become heavy metal, although his influences were anything but. Page also lent a hand in writing Led Zeppelin's vast array of classic songs and produced all their albums. Onstage, he was a consummate showman, sometimes getting bizarre sounds by using a viola bow to play his guitar while treating the sound with an Echoplex.

Page's career includes a stint with the Yardbirds, collaborations with Joe Cocker and Roy Harper, as well as his own, solo release. However his best work was done with Led Zeppelin, where his ability for developing strong melodies offset his brash but articulate guitar style, and he developed a breathtaking subtlety.

Although Page's guitar style draws heavily on the blues, also utilizes a range of styles that could be called music, with influences from North Africa, the Jamaica and elsewhere. Page took the blues, his tation along with Jeff Beck from the Yardbirds, and in tion from hard rock pioneers like Hendrix, and created his own distinctly powerful sound.

Although a sloppy lead player by modern standards, the feeling and attitude with which he plays each solo furthers the music better than if he were clinically precise. Regardless of any shortcomings in his technique, he has played some of the best and most famous guitar solos ever recorded. Page's leads were always very tasty, melodic and emotional.

GEAR

Guitars: Guitars: 1958 Gibson Les Paul Standard, Gibson ES-1275 doubleneck, 1958 Fender Telecaster.

Amps: Marshall Super Lead 100-watt stacks
Pedals: Roger Mayer Tonebender fuzz box, Vox Cry Baby Wah, Maestro Echoplex, MXR Phase 90

ESSENTIAL LISTENING
Dazed and Confused (Led Zeppelin – *Led Zeppelin*, 1969) • Whole Lotta Love, Heartbreaker (Led Zeppelin – *Led Zeppelin II*, 1969) • Since I've been Loving You (Led Zeppelin – *Led Zeppelin III*, 1970) • Kashmir (*Physical Graffiti*, 1975) • Rock and Roll, Stairway to Heaven (Led Zeppelin – *Untitled*, 1971) • Achilles Last Stand (Led Zeppelin – *Presence*, 1976)

ESSENTIAL VIEWING
Led Zeppelin (Led Zeppelin, 2003) • *The Song Remains The Same* (Led Zeppelin, 1976)

JOHN PETRUCCI
Dream Theater's John Petrucci is one of the most technically accomplished hard rock guitarists in contemporary music. Unlike many other guitar heroes of the late 1980s, he is not an instrumental solo artist.

Petrucci grew up on Long Island, New York, where he started playing guitar at the age of 12, and developed a love for progressive rock and heavy metal. His musical education began with a music theory class in high school. He is mostly self-taught, but did receive a few lessons when he attended Berklee College of Music in Boston, where he studied jazz composition and harmony.

Petrucci's love for lyric writing combined with his unique composing style of progressive fusion shape the sound of Dream Theater. His has recorded seven albums with the band, and has also been involved in several side projects.

Most electric guitarists do one thing extremely well, and ᵛⁱⁿd to play to their strengths. However, Petrucci does `ⁿ well: alternate and sweep picking; legato; two-ₚing; arpeggios and vibrato. He is also well ₕord theory, harmony, arranging and orchestra-ₑ is a well-rounded player who can incorporate different styles in his playing.

GEAR
Guitars: Ernie Ball Musicman John Petrucci signature 6- and 7-string electrics
Amps: Three Mesa Boogie Roadkings, Two Mesa Boogie Lonestars, Two 2x12 Mesa cabinets, Two 4x12 Mesa cabinets
Rack: TwoTC Electronic 2290, two TC Electronic M3000, TC Electronic G Force, Eventide DSP7000, DMC System Mix, DBX 266XL, Mesa High Gain Amp Switcher, Dunlop Cry Baby Custom Shop Rack Wah, Custom Mark Snyder interface, Furman AR Pro power regulator

ESSENTIAL LISTENING
Metropolis, Pt. 1, Take the Time (Dream Theater – *Images & Words*, 1992) • Lie, Scarred (Dream Theater – *Awake*, 1994) • When the Water Breaks (Liquid Tension Experiment – *Liquid Tension Experiment*, 1999) • This Dying Soul: IV (Dream Theater – *Train of Thought*, 2003)

ESSENTIAL VIEWING
Metropolis 2000: Scenes From New York (Dream Theater – 2000) • *Live at Budokan* (Dream Theater, 2004) • *Images and Words Live in Tokyo/5 Years in a Live Time* (Dream Theater – 2004)

CARLOS SANTANA
Santana fused Latin influences with West Coast rock, making him a fusion artist before the term was coined. He is best known as the leader of the band Santana, which has existed since the late 1960s. The band's first album, *Santana*, and their performance at Woodstock in 1969, exerted a strong influence, with many bands adding Latin percussion to their lineups.

In 1972 Santana took the lead from John McLaughlin and headed in a spiritual, jazz/fusion direction. From 1976 he still stretched out instrumentally, but included mainstream rock and dance elements, a combination he has maintained.

Santana usually releases an album every year, either under the band's name or his own. He will often collaborate with other musicians and constantly explores different styles of music to expand on his musical style.

While his live shows had a reputation for excellence, Santana did not have a major hit between 1981 and 1999, when he made a dramatic comeback with the album *Supernatural*, which was a series of collaborations with other artists such as Matchbox Twenty's Rob Thomas, Wyclef Jean, and Dave Matthews. *Supernatural* went platinum 25 times over and earned nine Grammy awards.

Santana is a very pure and passionate guitar player, and can create more tension with a guitar than most players. He has a unique tone and a distinctly intense voice. No matter who he is playing with, or whether he is playing rock, jazz, Latin or funk, he is always instantly recognizable as Santana.

GEAR
Guitars: PRS Santana models
Amps: 70's Marshall 100w head with a single 4 x 12" cab, '65 Blackface Fender Twin, MESA combo with 1 x 12" Altec speaker
Pedals: Wah, Ibanez TS-9 Tube Screamer

ESSENTIAL LISTENING
Jingo, Soul Sacrifice (Santana – *Santana*, 1969) • Black Magic

Woman/Gypsy Queen, Oye Como Va, Samba Pa Ti (Santana – *Abraxas*, 1970) • Batuka, No One to Depend On, Toussaint L'Overture, Guajira (Santana – *Santana III*, 1971)

ESSENTIAL VIEWING
Sacred Fire (Santana, 2001) • *Supernatural Live* (Santana, 2000)

JOE SATRIANI

Joe Satriani is one of the most technically accomplished and respected guitarists to emerge in recent times. His melodic compositions are both technically dazzling and easily accessible.

Born in New York in 1956, 'Satch' first picked up the guitar at the age of 14, inspired by guitar legend Jimi Hendrix. Quickly mastering the instrument, he was teaching guitar to others by 1971, including Steve Vai, who became a friend. He continued his studies with jazz greats Billy Bauer and Lennie Tristano. In 1978 Satriani moved to Berkeley, California. He continued teaching, and was an influential teacher to other rock guitarists like Metallica's Kirk Hammett, Larry LaLonde of Primus, Counting Crows' David Bryson, and jazz fusion player Charlie Hunter.

In 1986 Satriani released his first solo album, *Not of This Earth*. The timing was good, as Steve Vai had been praising Satriani in magazine interviews. In 1987 came his second album, *Surfing With The Alien*, amply showcasing his talents as composer, player and producer. The album became the most successful instrumental rock record since Jeff Beck's *Wired*, with sales of over a million copies in the USA alone. Satriani's face started showing up on the covers of major guitar magazines.

Satriani creates lyrical, melodically sophisticated instrumental music, but uses the structure of popular songs. This allows listeners to latch onto his soaring lyrical melodies before being dazzled by his advanced technique. His trademarks are a warm, bluesy tone, delicate phrasing and musicianship with a carefully applied dash of speed.

GEAR
Guitars: Various Ibanez JS (Joe Satriani) models
Amps: 100W Marshall 60 with Marshall 4 x 12 cabinet
Pedals: Jim Dunlop 535Q Wah, Boss DS-1 Distortion, Fulltone Ultimate Octave, DigiTech Whammy, Boss OC-2 Dual Octave, PS-5 Super Shifter Pedal, Boss BF-3 Flanger, Boss Super Chorus, Boss DD-2 Delay, Chandler Digital Delay

ESSENTIAL LISTENING
Always With Me Always With You, Satch Boogie (*Surfing

With The Alien, 1987) • The Forgotten Part Two, The Mystical Potato Head Groove Thing (*Flying in a Blue Dream*, 1989) • Why, Cryin' (*The Extremist*, 1992) • Love Thing (*Crystal Planet*, 1998)

ESSENTIAL VIEWING
G3 Live in Concert (G3, 2000) • *Live In San Francisco* (Joe Satriani, 2002)• *G3 Live in Denver* (G3, 2004)

BRIAN SETZER

Brian Setzer was born in New York City and raised on Long Island. When he was eight years old he took up the euphonium, which he played for 10 years. He at first took his inspiration from blues-rock bands like Led Zeppelin, although he also developed a keen interest in jazz and big band swing.

Setzer started forming rockabilly bands in the 1970s, putting together the Stray Cats in 1978. The band took the UK by storm, and then returned to the USA to convert audiences there. While on tour with the Stray Cats, Setzer practised jazz chords and listened to the recordings of big bands.

Following the demise of the Stray Cats, Setzer formed the Brian Setzer Orchestra, a 17-piece big band. When the big-band swing revival of the late 1990s took off, Setzer was at the forefront with his disc, *The Dirty Boogie*, and its hit single 'Jump, Jive an' Wail'. *The Dirty Boogie* garnered two Grammy awards.

Whether performing with the Stray Cats, the Brian Setzer Orchestra or the Brian Setzer Trio, he is the hard-rocking king of swing, with jazzy rockabilly, country and blues chops and a wonderful tone, brimming with rock and roll character.

Aside from his band projects, Setzer also keeps busy with TV and movie soundtracks, including tracks for Disney's *The Country Bears* and the *House of Mouse* cartoon series. He has also worked for artists such as Bob Weir, Bob Dylan, Stevie Nicks and Robert Plant.

GEAR
Guitars: 1959 Gretsch 6120, 1957 Fender Stratocaster, 1957 Gretsch Silver Jet, 1959 Gretsch 6119 Custom, 1955 Gretsch 6130, 1956 Gretsch 6129, 2001 Gretsch Brian Setzer Hot Rod Customs, 1957 Gretsch 6136 White Falcon
Amps: 1962 Fender Bassman, 1960 Fender Princeton
Pedals: Roland 301 Chorus Echo

ESSENTIAL LISTENING
Stray Cat Strut, Rock This Town (Stray Cats – *Built for Speed*, 1982) • The House Is Rockin' (Brian Setzer – *Guitar Slinger*, 1996) • Jump, Jive an' Wail, This Cat's on a Hot Tin Roof (Brian Setzer Orchestra – *The Dirty Boogie*, 1998)

ESSENTIAL VIEWING

Live in Japan (The Brian Setzer Orchestra, 2001) • *This Joint Is Jumpin'* (The Brian Setzer Orchestra, 1999) • *Rumble in Brixton* (Stray Cats, 2004)

JAMES 'MUNKY' SHAFFER

James Shaffer was born in Rosedale, California, on 6 June 1970. He began his musical career after an accident with his three-wheeler, which severed the top of his left index finger. Doctors advised that he take up a musical instrument to rehabilitate the finger, and Shaffer's first choice was the guitar.

Shaffer was in a band named LAPD with Head, David and Fieldy. After issuing a CD in 1993, they crossed paths with Jonathan Davis, a mortuary science student moonlighting as the lead vocalist for the local group Sexart. The band soon asked Davis to join the band and upon his arrival, the quintet rechristened itself Korn.

Korn's dark, heavy alternative metal sound made them among the most popular and provocative bands to emerge during the post-grunge era. They released their debut CD, *Korn*, in late 1994, and thanks to a relentless touring schedule that included opening for Ozzy Osbourne, Megadeth, Marilyn Manson and 311, the record slowly but steadily gained in popularity, eventually going gold. *Life Is Peachy* followed in 1996, and was a more immediate hit, reaching the number three spot on the pop album charts. The following year, they headlined the Lollapalooza tour, but dropped out when Shaffer contracted viral meningitis.

Shaffer uses the seven-string Ibanez Universe guitars tuned low (the 7th string is tuned to an A and the 6th to D, etc.), giving him a very heavy sound.

GEAR

Guitars: Ibanez UV-7 7-String Electric Guitar
Amps: Mesa/Boogie Triple Rectifier Head with Marshall 4x12 Cabinet
Pedals: Boss RV-3 Reverb Delay, Digitech XP-100 Whammy Wah, DOD FX-25 Envelope Filter, Dunlop UniVibe, Electro-Harmonix Big Muff Pi Distortion, Electro-Harmonix Electric Mistress Flanger, Electro-Harmonix Small Stone Phaser

ESSENTIAL LISTENING

Shoots and Ladders, Blind (Korn – *Korn*, 1994) • No Place to Hide, A.D.I.D.A.S (Korn – *Life is Peachy*, 1996) • It's On (Korn – *Follow The Leader*, 1998) • Here to Stay (Korn – *Untouchables*, 2002)

ESSENTIAL VIEWING

Korn: Live (2002) • *Korn – Deuce* (2002)

STEVE VAI

Steve Vai first stepped into the spotlight in 1980 as a guitarist in Frank Zappa's band. Zappa would introduce him as the 'little Italian virtuoso' and credit him with 'Impossible Guitar Parts' and 'Stunt Guitar'. He then moved to fill Yngwie Malmsteen's shoes in Alcatrazz. In 1985 he stepped into the most coveted position in the guitar world at the time: guitarist for David Lee Roth, who had just left Van Halen. In each role Vai showed that he had a phenomenal technique and unique sound as a guitarist, as well as impressive composition and arrangement skills.

Vai's biggest contribution to guitar came during his solo career. His debut, *Flex-Able*, was raw and quirky, but had moments of genius. This set the stage for his most influential and best-selling album, *Passion & Warfare*, which expanded the lexicon of rock guitar and ushered in an era of guitar virtuosos in the early 1990s.

Vai studied at Berklee School of Music in Boston and with guitar teacher/performer Joe Satriani. He practises religiously – 15 hours a day is not unusual. He follows Zappa's hard-working approach to composition and performance yet embraces the theatrics and dress fashion of heavy rock. His music is powerful, fast and dynamic.

Newer guitar idols like James 'Munky' Shaffer of Korn, Mike Einziger of Incubus and Tom Morello of Audioslave all cite Vai as a major source of inspiration.

GEAR

Guitars: Ibanez JEM and Universe electric guitars, which he helped design
Amp: Two Carvin Legacy 100Watt Heads, each with one Carvin Legacy cabinet
Pedals: Boss DS-1 Distortion, Boss FV-50H Stereo Volume Pedal, Digitech WH-1 Whammy, Morley Bad Horsie Wah
Rack effects: Eventide H3000/3500 Harmonizer, Roland SDE-3000 Digital Delay, TC Electronic Fireworx Multi-FX, TC Electronic G-Force Multi-FX

ESSENTIAL LISTENING

The Attitude Song (Steve Vai – *Flex-Able*, 1984) • Yankee Rose (David Lee Roth – *Eat 'Em and Smile*, 1986) • For the Love of God, The Audience is Listening (Steve Vai – *Passion & Warfare*, 1994) • Bad Horsie (Steve Vai – *Alien Love Secrets*, 1995)

ESSENTIAL VIEWING

Live at the Astoria London (Steve Vai, 2004) • *G3 Live in*

Concert (G3, 2000) • *G3 Live in Denver* (G3, 2004) • *Crossroads* (1986 feature film, plays the devil's guitarist)

EDDIE VAN HALEN

Eddie Van Halen was one of the most influential, original, and talented rock guitarists of the 20th century, second only to Jimi Hendrix. When his band, Van Halen, released their self-titled first album in 1978, it immediately changed the face of rock guitar forever.

Born in 1955 in the Netherlands, Eddie Van Halen started taking piano lessons at an early age, and was regarded as a prodigy. After the family moved to the United States in the 1960s, he began playing the guitar, while his brother Alex took up the drums.

The brothers began playing gigs in the Los Angeles area and hooked up with flamboyant singer David Lee Roth and bassist Michael Anthony in the early 1970s. By the middle of the decade this band was calling itself Van Halen. Around the same time Eddie Van Halen developed the technique of two-handed tapping, which soon became his trademark. With his awesome speed and phrasing, flashy pyrotechnics and precision, Eddie soon became the top guitarist on the local music scene.

Eddie also began custom-building his own guitars as he wanted to obtain a Gibson sound but with a Stratocaster's comfortable body and vibrato. He ended up using a Fender Stratocaster body with a single Gibson PAF pickup in the bridge position. He would also cover the body of his guitar in strips of electrician's tape, creating another trademark. He created his own line of guitars for the Ernie Ball Company in the early 1990s, before switching to Peavey in the mid-1990s.

GEAR
Guitars: Peavey Wolfgang model
Amps: Six Peavey 5150 EVH amps. Occasionally uses Marshall 100-watt Super-Lead or HiWatt heads.
Pedals: Boss OC-2 Octave, Boss SD-1 Super Overdrive, Custom Audio Electronics RS-10 Midi Foot Controller, Dunlop CryBaby Wah, MXR Phase 90 Phaser, MXR Stereo Flanger
Rack Effects: Custom Audio Electronics Amp Selector/ Router, Eventide H3000/3500, harmonizer, Lexicon PCM-70 Reverb, Palmer Speaker Simulator, Rockman Smart Gate Noise Gate, Roland SDE-3000 Digital Delay

ESSENTIAL LISTENING
Eruption (Van Halen – *Van Halen*, 1978) • Push Comes to Shove, Mean Street (Van Halen – *Fair Warning*, 1981) • Jump, Hot For Teacher (Van Halen – *1984*, 1984)

ESSENTIAL VIEWING
Video Hits, Vol. 1 (Van Halen, 1999)• *Live Without a Net* (Van Halen, 2004)

STEVIE RAY VAUGHAN

If there was ever a person more successful than Eric Clapton in popularizing the blues, it was Stevie Ray Vaughan. He was at the forefront of the blues revival in the 1980s, almost singlehandedly bringing the style back to popularity.

Vaughan first came to prominence when David Bowie hired him to play on the *Let's Dance* album (1983), having seen Vaughan and his band, Double Trouble, perform at the Montreux Jazz Festival, in Switzerland. Vaughan was signed up by legendary A&R man John Hammond, and it was with Double Trouble and the breakthrough 1983 album, *Texas Flood*, that Vaughan found success. Tracks such as 'Pride and Joy' and 'Lenny' began getting airplay on radio stations in 1983. From the first few bars, Vaughan's playing grabbed public attention. Guitar players, both blues and rock, immediately took notice of the Texan and his fiery playing style. *Texas Flood* was nominated for two Grammy Awards, and Vaughan won three *Guitar Player* Reader's Poll awards – a feat equalled only by Jeff Beck.

Vaughan never believed himself to be doing anything new, and paid tribute to his influences – rock players like Jimi Hendrix and Lonnie Mack, as well as blues masters like Albert King and Howlin' Wolf. However, he had fresh intensity and attitude, and for the next seven years – until his untimely death in an air crash in August 1990 – he redefined the sound of the blues.

Stevie Ray Vaughan was a powerful player and strung his Stratocaster with very heavy gauge (.013 – .058) strings. He tuned his guitar down one half-step (to Eb), as Hendrix did.

GEAR
Guitar: 1963 Fender Stratocaster with '59 pickups.
Amps: Two Fender Super Reverb Combos with 4 x 10 speakers, Two Fender VibroVerb Combos with 1 x 15 speakers
Pedals: Vox Wah, Two Ibanez TS808 Tube Screamers, UniVox UniVibe

ESSENTIAL LISTENING
Scuttle Buttin', Couldn't Stand the Weather, Tin Pan Alley (Stevie Ray Vaughan and Double Trouble – *Couldn't Stand the Weather*, 1984) • Testify, Rude Mood, Lenny (Stevie Ray Vaughan and Double Trouble – *Texas Flood*, 1983) • Chitlins Con Carne (Stevie Ray Vaughan and Double Trouble – *The Sky Is Crying*, 1991)

ESSENTIAL VIEWING

Live at Montreux 1982 & 1985 (Stevie Ray Vaughan and Double Trouble, 2004) • *Live at the El Mocambo 1983* (Stevie Ray Vaughan and Double Trouble, 1991) • *Live From Austin, Texas* (Stevie Ray Vaughan and Double Trouble, 1995)

ANGUS YOUNG

AC/DC guitarist Angus Young is one of the most energetic and entertaining performers in rock. This diminutive man in a schoolboy's uniform – his trademark since the band's early days – makes a Gibson SG look huge. From the moment he appears on stage, he never stops moving. He headbangs, runs around and plays solos while spinning around on his back – all while playing loud rock-and-roll riffs. On top of his electrifying stage performance, Young is one of the best stripped-down rock guitarists.

Angus and his brother Malcolm were influenced by blues guitarists like Chuck Berry and Muddy Waters, as well as British rock guitarists such as Keith Richards of the Rolling Stones and Pete Townshend of The Who. The brothers formed AC/DC in Australia in the early 1970s.

Young's school uniform is a reminder of AC/DC's early days; the band would practise after school, and Young would wear his uniform. It proved to be popular with the fans, so he kept it as part of his stage act.

Young claims that his reasons for constantly moving around on stage are that he has to throw his whole body into bending notes, and when he does this he overbalances and has to move to keep from falling over. Legend has it however, that it comes from an incident where he did trip on stage – and the audience loved it.

Even during the 1980s, when other guitarists were copying Eddie Van Halen, Angus Young stuck to his economical, blues-based playing style, and AC/DC remain as popular today as they have in the past.

GEAR

Guitars: Gibson SG
Amps: Live – Four Marshall 1959 SLP Plexi heads driving 8 Marshall 4 x 12" speaker cabs, loaded w/25W Celestion 'Greenback' speakers.
Studio – Marshall JTM 45 head

ESSENTIAL LISTENING

Whole Lotta Rosie (AC/DC – *Let There Be Rock*, 1977) • For Those About to Rock (AC/DC – *For Those About to Rock We Salute You*, DATE)• Highway to Hell (AC/DC – *Highway to Hell*, 1979) • Hell's Bells, Back In Black (AC/DC – *Back in Black*, 1980) • Problem Child (AC/DC – *Dirty Deeds Done Dirt Cheap*, 1981)

ESSENTIAL VIEWING

Rock Masters (AC/DC, 1977) • *Stiff Upper Lip Live* (AC/DC, 2000) • *Live at Donington* (AC/DC, 2003)

FRANK ZAPPA

Frank Zappa was arguably the most accomplished and important composer of the rock era, combining a wide range of influences, from classical composers through styles such as doo-wop, rock and roll and blues to rock. Zappa was a satirist with a wicked sense of humour and taste for the absurd. He was also the most prolific artist of his time, turning out over 60 albums in his lifetime, with enough unmixed material recorded for easily another 60.

During the 1960s, with his band The Mothers, Zappa developed a unique stage show that combined humour, theatre and music. This was refined in his solo efforts, becoming complicated rock shows with choreography and conducting.

Zappa's controversial lyrics often overshadowed his music, but there is enough complexity in his compositions for a lifetime of study. Polyrhythms and odd time signatures are coupled with complex arrangements and fast intricate melodies. The ability to use and parody any other style of music was used to full effect.

A demanding leader, Zappa's band was a training ground for top musicians, including many of today's best instrumentalists. As a soloist, Zappa used no stock phrases, but improvized in the true sense of the word, going on what was in his head at any moment. His solos were often chaotic, but had a complex logic when taken as a whole. Zappa did not make his playing look easy. However the sounds that came from his tortured technique were often transcendental.

GEAR

Guitars: Fender Stratocaster, Gibson SG, Gibson Les Paul
Amps: Marshall, Carvin, Seymour Duncan and Acoustic 100W Heads with a variety of cabs
Pedals: CryBaby Wah, Rat Distortion
Rack Effects: Roland GP-8, Mu-tron Bi Phase, two MXR digital delays, Electro Harmonix Big Muff,

ESSENTIAL LISTENING

Montana – (Frank Zappa – *Overnite Sensation*, 1973) • Inca Roads (Frank Zappa – *One Size Fits All*, 1975) • Zoot Allures (Frank Zappa – *Zoot Allures*, 1976) • Watermelon In Easter Hay (Frank Zappa – *Joe's Garage*, 1979) • Pink Napkins (Frank Zappa – *Shut Up and Play Yer Guitar*, 1981) • St. Etienne (Frank Zappa – *Jazz From Hell*, 1986)

ESSENTIAL VIEWING

Does Humor Belong in Music? (1984) • *Baby Snakes* (1979)

INDEX

maintenance and setup 93–107
Malmsteen, Yngwie 150–51
Marshall amplifiers 50, 51
Marshall and CBS 50–52
Marshall JTM 45 50
Marshall Twin Stack 54
Marshall, Jim 50
May, Brian 151
McCarty, Ted 12
McLaughlin, John 151–52
Mesa/Boogie amp 51
metronomes 75
microphone preamp 120
microphones 115
MIDI control (amp) 53
MIDI guitar 16, 17
mixdown 156
mixers, the 119
mixing 135
modelling 56
    guitars 18–19
    technology 53
modulation 77
monitor cabinet 125
monitor systems 123
Morello, Tom 152
Morrison, Sterling 26
multi-speaker cabinet 138
mute switches 122

Native Instruments Guitar Rig 52
neck 14, 15, 32, 34, 38
    joint 37
    relief, checking 99
    shapes 35
    wood 34, 35
nut 14, 15, 34
    action 102
    lowering 103
    measuring 102
    raising string height 103

Octave dividers 83
output 124
output groups 122
output socket 15
overdrive 82
overdubs 135

PA systems 114– 116
Page, Jimmy 67, 152–53
panning 88, 156
panoramic potentiometer (pan pot) 122
Parker 19
Parker Fly (guitar) 13, 24, 25
Parker, Ken 13
patch memories (amp) 53
patches 91
Paul Reed Smith 23, 42, 44
Paul, Les 11
Peavey Classic 5150 (amp) 55
Peavey Transformer 112 54

pedals vs rack units 79
peg winders 65 *see also* string winders
Petrucci, John 153
phase reverse 122
phase switches 47
phasers 81
picks 66 *see also* plectrums
pick-ups 10, 13, 14, 15, 38–39, 156
    active 16
    configurations 39
    DiMarzio 24
    electromagnetic 9
    humbucking 12, 22
    selector switches 46
    simple 11
    soapbar 12, 21
piezo saddles 19
piezoelectric crystals 19
pitch shifter 84
plectrums 66 see also picks
plugs 71, 72
polar patterns (mic) 115
pot 156
power adaptors 77
power rating and loudness 56
power requirements 77–78
pullback 156

Rack mounts 55
radius 156
recording (at home) 137–139
recording process, the 132, 133
rehearsing 110–111
reverberation 89
Rey, Alvino 10
Rickenbacker 360-12 23, 36
Rickenbacker, Adolph 9
Roland 53
Roland Jazz Chorus JC-120 (amp) 51
Roland VG-88 Models 53
Roland VGA-5 56, 59, 60
roller nuts 34
Rolling Stones 108
rotary potentiometers 47

Saddle, adjustment 104
Santana, Carlos 153–54
Satriani, Joe 154
scale length 14, 15, 38, 156
semi-hollow guitar 12
series/parallel switches 47
Setzer, Brian 154–55
Shaffer, James 'Munky' 155
shim 103, 156
Silverface Fender amp 51
six-note tuner 70
six-stud tremolo 44
sole switches 122
solid-body guitar 11, 20, 21
Soloist 13
speakers 57–58
stacked humbuckers 39

Steinberger 13 Guitar
Steinberger, Ned 13
Stick, Grand Stick 27
Stick, The 26–27
stomp box 156
stop tailpieces 43
straps, guitar 67
Stratocaster 16, 40
Stratocaster-style bridges 105
strings 26, 63, 64, 65
    cleaners 75
    construction 63
    gauge and tension 65
    lubricant 75
    retainers 34
    types 63
    winders 65 see also peg winders
    winding types 64
stringing 95–98
studios 126–131, 136
sustain 156
synthesizers, guitar 16, 17, 18
synthetic materials 19

Telecaster 11, 20, 120
Telecaster-style bridges 105
Thal, Ron 26
three-pick-up guitar 46
tone controls (amps) 47, 60
transducers 115
trapeze tailpiece 44, 156
travelling with guitars 106—107
truss rods 14, 15, 36, 99, 100
Tune-O-bridges 21, 43
Tune-O-Matic Gibson Les Paul 102
tuning machines 33
two-pick-up guitar 46
two-stud tremolo 45

Vai, Steve 24, 155–56
valve (tube) amplifiers 55
valve amps, proper care 60–61
Van Halen, Eddie 156
Vaughan, Stevie Ray 156–57
Vg-8 V-Guitar System 53
vibrato 12, 21, 85
Vigier Surfreter B›26
Vivi-Tone 9,
volume controls 46–47
volume pedal 87

Wah pedals 81
whammy bar 156
wireless in-ear monitors 125
wood, types used 25, 26, 34, 35, 36, 41,
wraparound tailpiece 44

Yamaha mixing desk 119
Young, Angus 157

Zappa, Frank 13, 26, 157
Ztar, The 27

PHOTOGRAPHIC CREDITS

All photography by Neil Hermann, with the exception of the photographers listed below and/or their agencies. (Copyright rests with the photographers and/or their agents.) **Key to locations**: t = top; b = bottom; l = left; r = right; c = centre. (No abbreviation is given for pages with a single image, or pages on which all photographs are by the same photographer.)

A = Arenapal
JB = Jen Bruce
DS/C = Digital Source/Creatas
LMA = Lebrecht Music & Arts
(TJ = Toby Jacobs; PC = Private Collection)

PA/P = Photo Access/Photonica
RM = Redfern Music Picture Library
(JA = Jorgen Angel; SC = Steve Catlin; JC = James Cumpsty; GD = Geoff Dann; RE = Richard Ecclestone; MH = Mick Hutson; BK = Bob King; RK = Robert

Knight; AL = Andrew Lepley; MOA = Micheal Ochs Archives; PP = Peter Pakvis; DR = David Redfern; NJS = Nicky J Sims; SS = Susan Stockwell; RV = Rob Verhorst; AW = Andrew Whittuck)
SL = Starr Labs

5..............................DS/C	22bl ....RM/SS	106 ....RM/RK
6 ....DS/C	22br ....LMA/PC	108 ....RM/RV
9 ....LMA/PC	23 ....RM/SC	109–110 ....PA/P
10 ....RM/MOA	24b ....LMA/PC	112 ....LMA/TJ
11t............................LMA/PC	26b ....JB	121 ....LMA/TJ
11b...........................RM/GD	27b ....SL	124 ....LMA/TJ
12b...........................RM/SC	31 ....LMA/PC	126 ....RM/AW
12t............................RM/DR	47 ....RM/SC	127 ....RM/NJS
13t............................RM/JA	50–51 ....LMA/PC	133 ....DS/C
13b...........................RM/SC	65 ....RM/RK	134 ....RM/AL
17–108 ....A	67 ....RM/DR	135 ....RM/JC
20 ....RM/SC	84–85 ....A	136 ....RM/MH
21 ....RM/RE	89 ....RM/AL	140 ....RM/BK

ACKNOWLEDGEMENTS

The author would like to extend his personal thanks to: Roy Viljoen, Newton Wetter, Steven Beak, Gareth Travis, Graham Andersen and everyone at Paul Bothner Music; Tully McCullagh and everyone at Spaced Out Sound Studios; Marty Hatlelid, Lea Rawlings and Dave Dunwoodie at Graph Tech Guitar Labs; Bumblefoot; Emmett Chapman; Greg Howard; Harvey Starr; Patrice Vigier; Marc Quigley at PRS Guitars; Justin Simpson; and Erika Gouws.